I0157527

FOUNDATIONAL
TRUTHS

A LAYMAN'S VIEW OF
MAJOR BIBLICAL EVENTS

Don L. Weidman

New Harbor Press

Copyright © 2019 Don L. Weidman

All rights reserved. No part of this publication may be reproduced, distributed or transmitted in any form or by any means, including photocopying, recording, or other electronic or mechanical methods, without the prior written permission of the publisher, except in the case of brief quotations embodied in critical reviews and certain other non-commercial uses permitted by copyright law. For permission requests, write to the publisher, addressed "Attention: Permissions Coordinator," at the address below.

New Harbor Press
1601 Mt Rushmore Rd, Ste 3288
Rapid City, SD 57701
www.newharborpress.com

Ordering Information:
Quantity sales. Special discounts are available on quantity purchases by corporations, associations, and others. For details, contact the "Special Sales Department" at the address above.

Foundational Truths/Weidman —1st ed.

ISBN 978-1-63357-366-6

First edition: 10 9 8 7 6 5 4 3 2 1

Scripture quotations are taken from the Holy Bible, King James Version (Public Domain).

Scripture quotations marked NKJV are taken from the New King James Version®. Copyright 1982 by Thomas Nelson, Inc. Used by permission. All rights reserved.

I would like to dedicate this book to my loving wife, Rebecca, who has encouraged me to write it and has been my cheerleader throughout the process. Without her, the work may never have been completed. Thank you, Becky.

Contents

Preface

My wife of sixty years, Rebecca Ruth ("Becky") has encouraged me to write this book for several years, and I have been able to resist until now. I have become aware that as we study the Word of God, we will learn the truths we find there. God will open up His Word to our understanding. We would be amiss if we do not share this newfound knowledge and pass it along to the next generation. Judges 2:10 states, "When all that generation had been gathered to their fathers, another generation arose after them who did not know the LORD nor the work which He had done for Israel."

Coupled with that, I am concerned with the amount of false teaching and misinformation that is available today to the young people as they attend public schools and universities. Brainwashing was always considered a part of warfare, but now it is prevalent in our society. We are in a battle for the minds of our young people and the next generation. Many churches and ministers are also falling into the deception. Specifically, the unproven theory of evolution, the gap theory, and the big bang theory are major attacks against the foundational truths of the Word of God. That's why I feel the necessity to write this book so the next generation can read for themselves and not just accept what some teacher or professor is saying. This book represents my viewpoint from a lifetime of Bible study. You may not agree with my views, but at least you should consider them, measuring them with the Word of God. If this book causes you to study the Word of God to a deeper degree than you have in the past, then this book is a success.

I have, as stated above, been a serious student of the Bible for fifty-nine years and a Sunday school teacher for over forty years, which during this period of time, some of my understanding of the Scriptures changed as I gained new insight and knowledge of the Word of God.

Many denominations, churches, and preachers are accepting things that are promoted by a spiritually deteriorating culture. We must lift up Jesus and the work He did at the cross. This book will start at the foundational truth that God created the heavens, the earth, and all that is in them in seven twenty-four-hour days. It will then cover whether the earth is young or old using the text of the Bible itself. Scientists are using different methods to measure the age of a rock that are unreliable. However, scientists do not have a problem picking up a rock and saying the age of the rock is seven billion years old. They say the universe is 16.5 billion years old, but they don't have the evidence to prove it to be true. False information can and has led many people and even denominations away from the foundational truths of the Bible. This is not limited to but includes such teachings concerning the creation of the world like the big bang theory, the theory of evolution, the gap theory, and other teachings. Others are teaching that there is no rapture of the church. They believe that we are in the tribulation right now. Thank God there are still ministers out there who are teaching and preaching the truth without compromise.

Another reason for writing this book is the change we are witnessing in our culture where the number of young people attending church has drastically decreased. Less than half of millennials attend church. I dare say if you ask the average person on the street a question from the Bible, that person would have no idea what you were talking about.

It is, therefore, for the reasons and concerns listed above, that I feel compelled to write this book. My prayer is that it will help those who read it to establish a foundation of believing in God's Word no matter what the so-called scientists and skeptics say.

Don Weidman
Sunday school teacher

CHAPTER 1

Day 1

There have been a lot of books written and a lot of sermons preached about the creation process. Many of them provide information that the Scriptures do not support. They have inserted statements allowing for evolution and even statements that allow for a creative process that leaves God out altogether. This fits the narrative taught in the public schools. It also fits the false premise of separation of church and state propagated today even though that is not mentioned in the American constitution at all. My desire is to shine some light on these misleading theories and let the foundational truths of the Bible stand and enlighten the readers so they are well versed to defend the Bible. This is a time when every part of our society is under attack from Satan and his helpers. We are definitely in spiritual warfare, and Satan is pulling out all the stops, using every weapon at his disposal to destroy and tear down the absolute truths in the Bible. His goal is to defeat Christians, the church, and God. His original goal has not changed, and that was and is to replace God so that all the world will worship Satan instead. He knows his time is short because Jesus defeated him at the cross, therefore, he is fighting hard to the end.

With that in mind, let's begin in the beginning with Genesis chapter 1. I will take each verse and elaborate on it and cover some of the false teachings I have run across in my studies.

> In the beginning God created the heavens and the earth. (Genesis 1:1)

If you will keep an open mind I will show you how most people read things (such as the gap theory, the theory of evolution and the big bang theory) into the Scriptures covering the creative week. First, I will cover how I think we should read the creation account.

Think of the vast empty space that became the universe. Our minds cannot comprehend the vastness of the universe, but it is a small thing for God. It might have been just a small area on His workbench where He was putting together a new creation. Of course, God is all powerful and all knowing, and all He has to do is speak and the earth comes into existence. In fact, that is exactly what God did. He spoke the heavens and the earth into existence. Some people have an issue with the fact that God can speak and something can be created from nothing, but the Scriptures bare this out. Revelation 19:11–15 states:

> And I saw heaven opened, and behold a white horse; and He that sat upon him was called Faithful and True, and in righteousness He doth judge and make war. His eyes were as a flame of fire, and on His head were many crowns; and He had a name written, that no man knew, but He Himself. And He was clothed with a vesture dipped in blood: and His name is called The Word of God. And the armies which were in heaven followed Him on white horses, clothed in fine linen, white

and clean. And out of His mouth goeth a sharp
sword, that with it He should smite the nations.

The Scriptures here depict a future battle between Jesus (the
Word) and the nations gathered at the battle of Armageddon in
an attempt to destroy the nation of Israel. Jesus will not use tanks
or conventional weapons to defeat these nations but rather will
speak and the nations will be annihilated. But how? For the answer to that question, we must go to Ezekiel 38:22. God will defeat Gog, the leader of Magog, in the final battle of Armageddon:

> "And I will bring him to judgment with pesti-
> lence and bloodshed; I will rain down on him,
> on his troops, and on the many peoples who are
> with him, flooding rain, great hailstones, fire, and
> brimstones" (Ezekiel 38:22).

Verse 23 identifies this as the last battle because it shows that
the nations will finally know that Jesus is the King of kings and
Lord of lords. Revelation 16:21 also verifies the hailstones as a
weapon the Lord will use to defeat his enemies:

> "And great hailstones from heaven fell upon men,
> each hailstone about the weight of a talent."

A talent is about one hundred pounds. Revelation 14:20 tells
us that the blood will flow as deep as the horse's bridle. Then
Ezekiel 39 describes how long it will take for the cleaning up of
the weapons and the bodies of the dead. God is all powerful, and
speaking something into existence is not a problem for Him. He
did not have to start with matter to create the planets and stars;
He just spoke them into existence. In Matthew 14:13–21, Jesus
did not find it an insurmountable problem to feed five thousand
men plus women and children with two fish and five loaves of

bread. The disciples had trouble believing it could happen, so Jesus had an object lesson for them by having each disciple (twelve in total) carry off a basket of leftovers.

Here is where I differ from scientists that espouse the big bang theory. Notice that God started with the earth as his first created object in space. He first created the space, then created the earth in it. There was no sun, moon, stars, or planets in verse 1, just the earth. Why would God start with the earth and not some great solar system or one of the great stars that is thousands of times larger than the earth? I believe that God had a special thing He wanted to accomplish on the earth. God was going to create human beings in the image of God and give them a free will so they could choose to glorify Him. God desired to have fellowship with mankind.

I will explain it this way. When I was a young boy, my brother and I received train sets for Christmas. They were both American Flyer trains and would puff smoke when they were running around the tracks. After a time of running our trains around the oval track, we got bored and decided to build a larger layout. Our father allowed us to set up some saw horses in the basement, and we put sheets of plywood on them to make an area for our new train layout. I got the privilege of carrying buckets of dirt down into the basement to build our mountain. We had a small town of plastic houses and businesses along with street lights that actually lit up. When we got the town and the mountain finished, we had a town with miniature people, a trestle for the train to climb the mountain, and a switching yard for the trains to switch to a different set of tracks. The mountain even had a lake at the top thanks to my Mother's baking pan. My point is this: It was great fun building the layout, and we worked hard on it for several weeks. After it was finished, we also got bored with this layout just like we did with the oval track in the beginning. I remember daydreaming about how nice it would be if I could just be small enough to walk down the street in that town and be the engineer on one of those trains. I wouldn't be bored anymore. It would be fun to operate the train while climbing the mountain my brother and I made. I would become part of our creation.

God had plans from the very beginning to become part of His creation. Remember, God is all knowing, and He knew from the foundation of the earth that Adam and Eve were going to fail and would be in need of a Savior. God was going to place Himself on the earth and become that Savior, because there was no one who could provide the perfect sacrifice that was required to redeem mankind. So, you see, the earth has a special importance above all the planets, stars, and solar systems in the universe. It's where God became one of us, and without His intervention, we would all be lost and without hope. John 3:16 says,

> "For God so loved the world (not the universe) that He gave His only begotten Son, that whoso-ever believes in Him should not perish but have everlasting life."

Yes, God wanted to walk down the streets of the cities and towns of His creation. He wanted to drive the train just like I wanted to. He wanted to feel what we feel. Most of all, God wants our fellowship and our worship to glorify Him.

Let's go back to Genesis 1:1: "In the beginning God created the heaven and the earth." After the creation of the earth, if you could have stood a great distance from it, you would not have been able to see it because it was in total darkness. There was no light. There was no sun, moon, or stars—no light at all. Dark as a coal mine at midnight.

Some years ago, my wife and I traveled to Chicago and went to a museum that had a coal mine below it, and you could take an elevator down to see what it was like working in the mines. When we got off the elevator, the guide told us he was going to turn off the lights so we could see what complete darkness is like. When he turned the lights off, you could hold your hand in front of your face and could not see it. What a weird feeling that was. You could feel the darkness. Well, that was what it must have been like at the beginning of the creation—complete absence of light.

Universe with no Light

Earth is there, but is not visible

Fig. 2. The universe at creation (Genesis 1:1).

The earth was without form and void; and darkness was on the face of the deep. And the Spirit of God was hovering over the face of the waters. (Genesis 1:2)

There is a lot of information in this second verse, and it is here that many ministers and denominations get sidetracked. There is a method to the creation events depicted in the Bible that would do one good to observe. When God performed a creative act and it is stated in a verse, the verse following clarifies and adds information to the verse above. Verse 2 clarifies what the earth looked like right after God created the earth in Genesis 1:1. Scripture explains Scripture if we will only study enough to understand what the Word of God says.

First, notice that the earth was totally covered with water, and as I said earlier, it was totally dark as verified in verse 2. I call the earth at this point "the blue earth" because the water covered the earth's surface. The Holy Spirit, the third person of the Trinity, was present and hovering over the waters.

Because the earth was covered with water, the features of the earth were not visible, meaning you would not see any mountains or other features. All that would be visible to the eye would be a sphere covered with water. That's the way I read Genesis 1:1–2. I just take the Bible word for word, nothing added.

These two verses are some of the most controversial in the Bible. This is where the gap theory is inserted and millions of years added so the church could have an answer for the theory of evolution. When Charles Darwin published his book *Origin of Species* in 1859 and it was accepted as revolutionary by the scientific community, the church was not prepared for the proposition that it took millions of years for the earth to form and for life to come into existence. Also, how were they going to handle the dinosaurs that the scientists say died out sixty million years ago?

The Gap Theory

The gap theory was a convenient way for church theologians to compromise with Darwin's theory and keep the Genesis account intact. If there was a gap between Genesis 1:1 and 1:2, evolution could have occurred over millions of years, and dinosaurs could have lived there too. Scientists today say the earth and the universe are about 16.5 billion years old. It really upsets me when a scientist picks up a rock and says that it is seven billion years old. Now that's real empirical data, isn't it. Scientists have no way of knowing exactly how old the earth is, and carbon dating is only accurate to approximately forty five hundred years. Those who know their Bible know the earth is no more than six thousand years old. I will prove that in a later chapter when we cover the age of the earth.

The problem with the gap theory is death, among other misrepresentations. If people and animals (dinosaurs too) lived millions or billions of years ago and God in Genesis 1:1 and 1:2 was recreating the earth, then death existed before Adam and Eve sinned, but the Scriptures clearly teach that death entered the world because of the original sin. Romans 5:12 says,

> "Therefore, just as through one-man sin entered the world, and death through sin, and thus death spread to all men, because all sinned."

We find ourselves in disagreement with the old earth ideology because you cannot have death existing before God said it did. There are many more proofs that the earth is approximately six thousand years old and not billions of years old.

I believe in the young earth, which is approximately six thousand years old. In fact, if you go through the genealogies of the Bible, you can see that it is not an old earth but rather was created about six thousand years ago.

In the last fifty years, scientists have developed technology that has in turn developed a test that helps prove that the earth came into existence very fast and not over a period of millions or billions of years. Scientists discovered Polonium P218. Polonium is an element in granite that disappears or dissipates within three minutes unless it is somehow trapped or encapsulated. Scientists have discovered Polonium locked in granite, which means the granite had to solidify within a three-minute period of time for the Polonium to be present. Since granite is the bedrock of the earth, that means the earth had to be formed within three minutes.

So much for the millions of years for evolution to occur. You see, the theory of evolution, and it is just a theory and never proven to be true, needs millions or billions of years to be believable. If evolution occurred rapidly, we would have all sorts of examples of creatures, and humans, in various evolutionary stages. We don't, so they must claim that it occurred over millions of years and is not visible to the observer. What a cop out! Have you ever noticed when Satan wants you to believe his lies, he always uses time with such small changes that you cannot observe and discern the changes he says take place? He just wants you to accept the lie.

That's how he keeps the lie of evolution going, and that is how he will keep the lie of climate change going. We can have one of the coldest winters in history and his cohorts (activists, scientists, and teachers) tell us that doesn't matter, the earth is warming. Politicians will use this farce to extract billions of dollars in the form of carbon taxes from the public and businesses without changing the climate one iota. The climate is in God's hands and His control.

In Revelation, God has recorded changes in the earth's weather during the tribulation, and there is no way humans can change what is going to happen. If humans could change the weather, then God's Word would be rendered incorrect. If God is incorrect about the weather, then what else has He gotten wrong? If He is wrong, then He can't be God.

Well, back to the gap theory. The church fathers definitely made a mistake in compromising with the scientific community in the mid-1800's.

Today, all you need to do is turn on your television and the first thing you see and hear, even in the cartoons your children watch on TV, is millions and millions of years ago. Folks, our children are being brainwashed in the classrooms, and we are too. If you don't believe it, just turn on the Discovery Channel or the History Channel, and they will tell you the earth is 16.5 billion years old and that the dinosaurs died out sixty million years ago.

Another theory the scientists are pushing and is accepted as truth without proof is the big bang theory.

The Big Bang Theory

The so-called "learned scientists" believe the universe came into existence when there was an explosion far out in the universe. This is called the big bang theory. Yes, they say the universe started with an explosion of some sort of matter in outer space. They can't tell you where the original material came from that caused the explosion, but you can be sure that God had nothing to do with it as far as they are concerned. Their theories are all godless theories. Do you see the difference in their theory versus the Bible's explanation? They don't begin with creation of the earth but instead with some unknown matter in outer space. The earth is of no special importance to them. I contend that the earth and mankind were and are of upmost importance to God. Why would He send His Son Jesus Christ to die on a cruel cross to redeem mankind from their sinful nature if He did not value mankind? John 3:16 states,

> "For God so loved the world, that He sent His only begotten Son, that whosoever believeth in Him should not perish, but have everlasting life."

Outer space is a space that consists of a vacuum. Now, when I worked in the automotive lighting industry, we had a machine called a vacuum metalizing machine. It was used to coat parts with a bright aluminum material so the product we were making would reflect light like a mirror. We would place the part to be coated in the chamber, place a small piece of aluminum foil on a heating element, then pump all the air out, creating a vacuum. When the heating element was turned on, there was a flash, and the aluminum foil vaporized and covered the entire part with a thin layer of aluminum. My point is this. In a vacuum, particles travel in a straight line.

If there was an explosion like the scientists say, then all the particles would travel in a straight line, and they would still be traveling in a straight line today after all those so-called billions of years.

When we look at what God created, we find solar systems and galaxies that have planets in orbit around suns and moons in orbit around the planets. It is just as if a mastermind, a creator, placed them in precise orbits. In fact, in our solar system, we have planets where their orbits are so precise that scientists today can calculate (thanks to Kepler and others) their exact location years in the past or years in the future with mathematics. How do you think NASA can send spacecraft to distant planets? The mathematics are precise. Explosions are not that precise. Sorry to say, but our scientists have gone so far out on a limb that they can't get back.

Another interesting piece of information, and I think God did this on purpose when He created the universe, is that the planets in our solar system rotate counterclockwise except for the planet Venus, which rotates clockwise. Now isn't that just like God to see down the path of time and see that scientists are going to say He had nothing to do with creation, it was just a big bang, and God decided to rotate one planet the other direction. How do they explain that?

One last word on evolution. The scientist working directly with Charles Darwin was a German scientist named Ernst Haeckel who falsified much of what they called "evidence" for evolution. It was proven false, but it took the scientific community another one hundred years to admit it. Even with that, the false information is still in our textbooks today. The brainwashing continues to this day and has even intensified with the advent of television and the Internet.

So, the bottom line is this: God created the heavens and the earth, and the earth was covered with water, and that's why it had no form. It was also void of all life. There were no fish, animals, or humans living on the earth. There were no plants, trees, or vegetation, just water.

> Then God said, 'Let there be light' and there was
> light. (Genesis 1:3)

God in His creative acts spoke and it happened. It didn't take millions of years; it happened when He spoke. When the servants at a wedding feast were instructed by Jesus' mother to do what Jesus says, they brought containers of water to Jesus because they ran out of wine, did Jesus say that it was going to take a long time because it has to go through the fermentation process? No! He spoke and wine appeared in the vessels. Not only was there wine in the vessels, but those at the wedding feast said the best wine had been saved until last (John 2:1–10). If Jesus is truly the creator of the universe, as I believe He is and Scripture says He is, then speaking a planet or planets into existence immediately is not a problem. Consider John 1:1–3 where it states,

> "In the beginning was the Word, and the Word
> was with God, and the Word was God. The same
> was in the beginning with God. All things were
> made by Him; and without Him was not anything
> made that was made."

When scientific theories are presented, the scientific community requires empirical evidence to prove or disapprove the theory. Scientists say they want empirical proof, yet they break their own rules and accept the theory of evolution as truth when there is yet no proof humans evolved from a monkey or originated from a one-celled creature in the goo. Now Christians should be intelligent enough to believe what God says in His Word rather than a few misguided scientists with manmade theories they cannot prove. Romans 1:20 states that God has evidence right before our eyes when He says,

> "For the invisible things of Him from the creation
> of the world are clearly seen, being understood by
> the things that are made, even His eternal power
> and Godhead; so that they are without excuse."

Who is without excuse? The unbelievers. We must accept what God says in His Word by faith just the same as unbelievers accept by faith what the scientists, teachers of evolution, the gap theory, and climate change do.

Back to Genesis 1:3. Keep in your mind, the universe was a great expanse of empty space, except for the earth, and it was in total darkness. There was no sun, moon, or stars to give out their light.

It is my belief that God, in verse 3, was creating light itself, just like He might create gravity or electricity. Remember, when Sir Isaac Newton discovered gravity, it was already in existence. When electricity was discovered, it was already in existence as well. Men just discovered gravity and electricity and began to understand how to harness them and make them useful for mankind.

Now look at verse 4 and see how it clarifies verse 3:

> And God saw the light, that it was good: and God
> divided the light from the darkness. (Genesis 1:4)

Light did not exist until God created it. God saw the light and said it was good. I believe light was everywhere at that instant or at least until He divided the light from the darkness in verse 4. There were no shadows because light was everywhere.

God called the light Day, and the darkness He
called Night. And the evening and the morning
were the first day. (Genesis 1:5)

We have here in the first five verses, the first day of creation
where God has created the earth and the heavens; He has created light and divided the light from darkness. He also named the
light as day and the darkness as night. Remember, the earth was
the only created heavenly body in existence at this time. It appeared as a totally blue sphere in space as it was covered entirely
with water. Since there was no sun or stars to provide the light, I
believe God himself was the light illuminating the universe. You
see, there will come a time when God again will be the light that
shines, and there will be no need for the sun. This is evident in
Revelation 22:5,

"There shall be no night there: They need no lamp
nor light of the sun, for the Lord God gives them
light."

This will occur in the future when the new Jerusalem comes
down to earth from heaven. By the way, the new Jerusalem will
be huge. It will be 1500 miles square and 1500 miles high. Think
about that and Jesus will be the light meaning we will not need
the sun or moon for light.

This light was shone to Peter, James, and John when Jesus took
them up on the mountain of transfiguration in Matthew 17:1–2:

"Now after six days, Jesus, and John his brother,
led them up on a high mountain by themselves;
and He was transfigured before them. His face
shone like the sun, and His clothes became as
white as the light."

So, to sum up the first day of creation, God created the heavens (the void of outer space) and the earth, which was entirely covered with water. God then created light and divided it into day (light) and night (darkness). Also notice that we did not add the gap theory or the big bang theory into the Word of God; we just took the Word as it is written. Concerning the water, I will explain that in day 2.

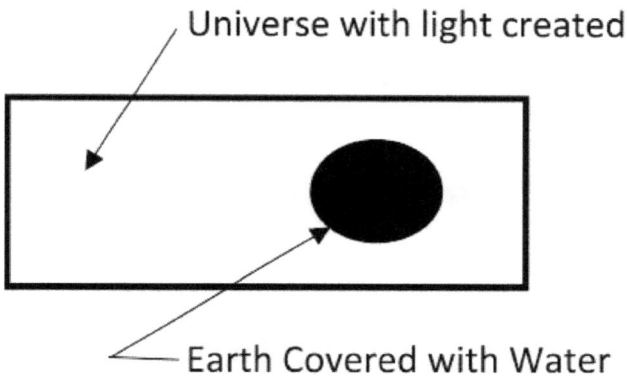

Universe with light created

Earth Covered with Water

Fig. 3. The earth covered with water in Genesis 1:2.

CHAPTER 2

Day 2

Then God said, Let there be a firmament in the
midst of the waters, and let it divide the waters
from the waters. (Genesis 1:6)

H ere we have God separating the waters from the waters. No, we are not talking about dry land. The land is
still completely under water after God separated the
waters. What we have here is water being lifted up forming a
sphere around the earth, and since it is most likely eighteen to
twenty miles up in space, it froze into a solid sphere of crystal-
clear ice. What you have is a sphere (the earth) encapsulated
within a sphere of ice with a void between the ice and the earth
called a firmament. We call it the atmosphere. How do we know
it is a sphere of ice? When I was on an airplane flying to Califor-
nia, the pilot came on the intercom and said, "Ladies and gen-
tlemen, we are at our cruising altitude of thirty-three thousand
feet, and the temperature outside is negative fifty-five degrees.
Water freezes at thirty-two degrees; therefore, we can be pretty
certain this water froze into a sphere of ice.

Now let's consider how deep the water was that covered the
earth in verse 1. To find that out, we must go to Genesis 7 where
we have the flood that destroyed the earth called Noah's flood.

The figure below depicts what occurred when God separated the waters.

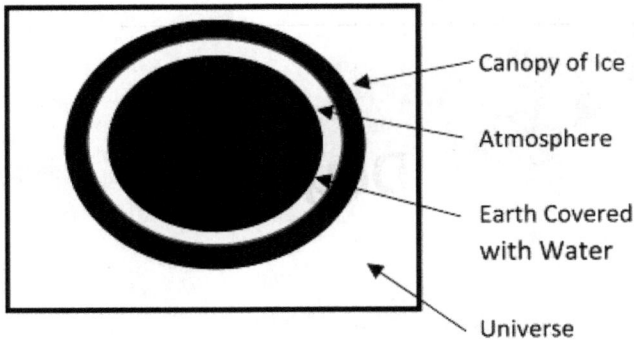

Fig. 4. The earth encapsulated within a sphere of ice (Genesis 1:6).

> The waters prevailed fifteen cubits upward, and the mountains were covered. (Genesis 7:20)

A cubit is a measurement from the tip of a man's finger to the elbow and can vary from eighteen to twenty-four inches. If we use the eighteen-inch measurement and multiply it by fifteen cubits, we get twenty-two feet, six inches, which is the depth of the water over the tallest mountain. Mount Everest is the tallest mountain on earth and measures 29,141 feet above sea level. Adding twenty-two feet, six inches to the height makes the water 29,163.5 feet deep at the time of creation.

In our drawing, we are showing Mount Everest as the large mountain at the right of the drawing in Figure 5. We show the depth of the water at the time of creation as measured from sea level since all elevations are measured from sea level. This is the depth of 29,163 feet, 6 inches. When God separated the waters creating a firmament or atmosphere, the water level dropped

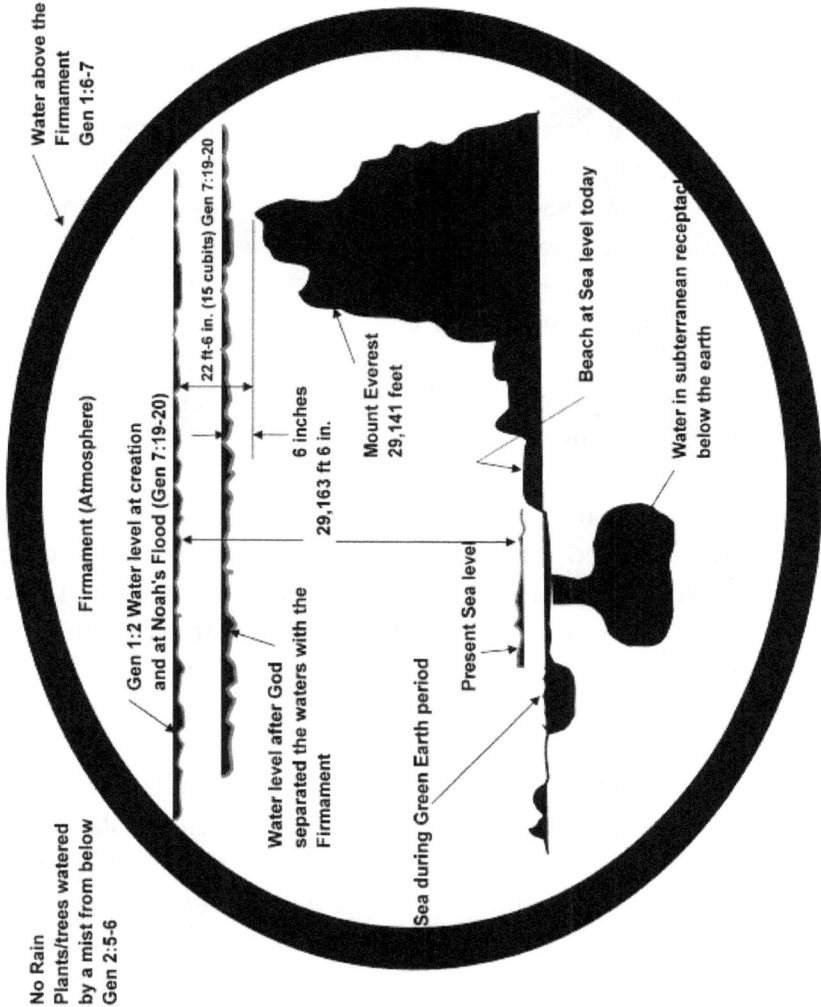

Fig. 5. Water depth with the ice canopy in place.

but still covered the highest mountain because there was still no land visible on the earth. I have shown six inches of water over Mount Everest so that we are still in agreement with the Scriptures. It could have been more or less in depth. The water that God separated above the firmament formed a sphere of frozen water around the earth as shown by the ellipse in the drawing. Remember, water does not disappear or leave the earth, so I contend that the original water that was there on creation day is still here today.

Let me say at this point that some will say there were no mountains as high as Mount Everest at that time; so therefore, the water could not have been that deep. They say the mountains were formed at the time of Noah's flood when there was a great upheaval in the earth causing continents to slide away from each other, mountains to form, and volcanic eruptions to take place, which melted the ice sphere encompassing the earth. I contend that the Bible says the water was fifteen cubits above the highest mountain because there was no dry land at that time in the creation week. So, yes, the water could have been lower in depth depending on what elevation the highest mountain was, but remember, when God separated the water causing some to go up and form the canopy that totally encapsulated the earth, there was still enough water left on earth so that no dry land was visible. The water depth over the highest mountain might only have been six inches after the separation of the water, but the mountains were still covered with water.

What was God doing? He was creating an ecosystem that was perfect for the earth and the inhabitants, which He would create later in the week. You see, the world we live in is under the curse (after Adam and Eve sinned in the garden in Genesis 3), and it is hard for us to comprehend and visualize what it was like after God finished with the creation of the earth and all that was in it. It was a perfect creation, a perfect ecosystem.

The sphere of ice that surrounded the earth was a filter that filtered out all of the damaging rays from the sun and at the same time diffused the light and heat so the earth would have a uniform temperature of around 72 degrees Fahrenheit year-round. There were no oceans, just small seas of fresh water; nor were there ice caps at the North and South Poles because the uniform temperature prevented ice from forming.

There was no rain on the earth according to Genesis 2:5–6 where it states,

> "[A]nd every plant of the field before it was in the earth, and every herb of the field before it grew: for the Lord God had not caused it to rain upon the earth, and there was no man to till the ground. But there went up a mist from the earth, and watered the whole face of the ground."

This tells us it did not rain on the earth. God watered the plants from a mist that rose up from the earth. In fact, it did not rain on the earth until Noah's flood.

The atmospheric pressure on the earth was another factor of the original creation that had a dramatic effect on the earth, plants, and mankind. The ice sphere caused the atmospheric pressure to increase to twice what it is today. Atmospheric pressure today is 14.7 pounds per square inch (psi). At creation when the ice sphere was in place, the atmospheric pressure would have been approximately 32 psi. The result of this higher atmospheric pressure was that an animal or a human would take in a larger amount of oxygen as today, making that animal or person stronger, healthier, and larger and providing a longer life. Today when you take a breath of air, you get about twenty-one percent oxygen, but at the time of creation, under twice the atmospheric pressure, you would draw in thirty percent oxygen with each breath. That would cause one to have tremendous energy levels, and the bodies of animals and humans would grow larger. Plants would be in abundance all over the earth. Since all the animals were vegetarian, as were the humans, plants had to be in abundance to feed the population (Genesis 1:29–30).

I saw how atmospheric pressure affected plants when I visited Biosphere 2 south of Tucson, Arizona. One part of Biosphere 2 was divided into three sections with the ability to control the atmospheric pressure separately in each section. The scientists at Biosphere 2 planted cottonwood cuttings, taken from the same mother tree, in each section. Each section of Biosphere 2 was under a different atmospheric pressure. The first section had one atmosphere of pressure like we live under today, while the second section had two atmospheres of pressure (approximately 32 psi). The third section had three atmospheres of pressure.

The results showed that the first section had cottonwood trees growing just like they would if planted outside (one atmosphere of pressure) today. The second section of trees under two atmospheres of pressure grew rapidly, outgrowing both the other two sections. The test showed that three atmospheres of pressure did not do as well as two atmospheres of pressure. God knows what He is doing. He knows what is best for His creation. Two atmospheres of pressure are ideal for humans and animals to live and thrive in.

Consider how the higher atmospheric pressure might affect your health. When a deep-sea diver comes up too fast, that person gets the bends because Nitrogen builds up in the joints and muscles. The diver must enter a decompression chamber where the pressure is raised to a point where oxygen is forced into the cells driving out the nitrogen. Medical doctors have discovered that patients with wounds that will not heal will begin to heal at a rapid rate under these conditions. They place the patient in a hyperbolic pressure chamber, where the high pressure promotes healing. That's precisely what the earth's atmosphere did at the time of creation. It aided one's health.

Earth's Orbit at Creation

As stated above, the earth did not have ice caps because of the uniform temperature around the entire planet. This occurred because the earth was not wobbling through space as it is today. Today, the earth's orbit is elliptical and wobbling, causing the earth to tilt away from the sun in winter and tilt more vertical in the summer. This is like a toy top slowing down as it spins and becoming less stable, thus the wobbling effect.

At creation, God established the earth's orbit as a perfect circle. When a top is set spinning, it will at first spin with such precision that its axis will be vertical and it will be stable, but shortly as it slows down, it will begin to wobble and eventually fall.

At creation, God established the rotation and orbit of the earth as a circle around the sun; therefore, one full three-hundred-sixty-degree rotation around the sun represented a year, and one degree represented one day. The earth was also spinning three hundred sixty degrees in twenty-four hours, constituting one day. God established a thirty-day month with twelve thirty-day months, making one year. We call a three-hundred-sixty-day year a prophetic year, which God established according to Genesis 7:11–13; 8:2–4.

Prophesies in the Bible and events such as Noah's flood prove this to be the case.

> In the six hundredth year of Noah's life, in the second month, the seventeenth day of the month, the same day were all the fountains of the great deep broken up, and the windows of heaven were opened. And the rain was upon the earth forty days and forty nights. In the selfsame day entered Noah, and Shem, and Ham, and Japheth, the sons of Noah, and Noah's wife, and the three wives of his sons with them, into the ark. (Genesis 7:11–13)

Notice they entered the ark on the seventeenth day of the second month. God established the exact time they entered the ark. Now look at Genesis 8:2–4:

> The fountains also of the deep and the windows
> of heaven were stopped, and the rain from heaven
> restrained; And the waters returned from off the
> earth continually: and after the end of the hun-
> dred and fifty days the waters were abated. And
> the ark rested in the seventh month, on the sev-
> enteenth day of the month, upon the mountains
> of Ararat.

We learn from these verses how God measured time and what His calendar looked like. From the seventeenth day of the second month to the seventeenth day of the seventh month is exactly five months. Verse 3 tells us this is one hundred fifty days or thirty days for each month. If every month has thirty days, then a year consists of three hundred sixty days, meaning the earth at creation and up to the flood of Noah rotated around the sun one degree for every twenty-four-hour day, or a perfect circle.

I know this is a lot to digest, but consider that God created the earth in perfect condition circling the sun in a perfect orbit, not wobbling. The time to orbit the sun would be three hundred sixty days instead of three hundred sixty-five days presently. By not wobbling, the axis of the earth would remain vertical, and the North and South Poles would be inhabited by humans and animals just like the rest of the earth. Because there would be no glancing rays of the sun, which occur today when the earth is tilted , and with the earth encased in the ice sphere, the earth's temperature would be 72 degrees Fahrenheit all around, even to the North and South Poles. This is why they have found mammoths in the Arctic still standing upright but frozen with food in their stomachs consisting of green vegetation. How could an animal become frozen while still standing and with vegetation in its stomach unless this change in climate occurred very rapidly?

The earth at the time of the flood with the ice canopy collapsing (coming down as rain) and the earth knocked out of its original orbit and wobbling could in fact cause a quick freeze of the poles.

In fact, I believe the earth was almost totally green with vegetation, as viewed from outer space, from creation until the flood. Why? Because humans and animals alike were vegetarians according to Genesis 1:29 (NKJV):

> And God said, "See, I have given you every herb that yields seed which is on the face of all the earth, and every tree whose fruit yields seed; to you it shall be for food. Also, to every beast of the earth, to every bird of the air, and to everything that creeps on the earth, in which there is life, have given every green herb for food.

Animals did not kill animals, and humans did not kill animals for food. Not until after the flood did this change occur where animals killed each other and humans killed animals for food.

> And the fear of you and the dread of you shall be on every beast of the earth, on every bird of the air, on all that move on the earth, and on all the fish of the sea. They are given into your hand. Every moving thing that lives shall be food for you. I have given you all things, even as the green herbs. (Genesis 9:2–3 (NKJV))

So, you see, God established a vegetarian diet for all of humankind and all of the animals, and not until after the flood did humans' and animals' diets change to eating flesh. Consider why the whole earth needed to be covered with vegetation. If humans and beasts were vegetarian and lived long lives as the Bible tells us in the genealogies, the population of the earth up until the time of the flood could have been as much as seventeen billion

humans. You can find graphs on the Internet showing the expo-
nential growth of the earth's population before the flood. Today's
population is about seven billion people, and we seem to have
problems providing enough food for them. Just think, if there
were seventeen billion people living on earth, how many animals were on the earth? It would require a larger land mass than
we see today to provide enough vegetation for them. Dinosaurs
would have existed during this time and would have been huge
eaters of vegetation.

Back to the creation events in Genesis 1:7, we find verse 7 is
descriptive of verse 6.

> Thus God made the firmament and divided the
> waters which were under the firmament from the
> waters which were above the firmament. (Gen-
> esis 1:7 (NKJV))

The firmament here would be our atmosphere where the
birds fly, and I figure this would go up about one hundred thousand feet (nineteen miles). Above that would be the ice sphere,
which could be about eleven feet thick.

> And God called the firmament Heaven. So, the
> evening and the morning were the second day.
> (Genesis 1:8 (NKJV))

There are three heavens mentioned in the Bible:

> I knew a man in Christ above fourteen years ago,
> (whether in the body, I cannot tell; or whether
> out of the body, I cannot tell: God knoweth;) such
> an one caught up to the third heaven. (2 Corinthi-
> ans 12:2)

The apostle Paul was caught up into the third heaven where God's throne is located. The second heaven is outer space, and the first heaven is the atmosphere here on earth. Earth has a special importance to God in that He even numbers the heavens starting here on earth. God called the atmosphere "heaven."

At the end of the second day, a major change has taken place in that the earth is now contained within a sphere of ice that incubates the earth, giving it a uniform temperature, and allows the whole surface of the earth support green vegetation, although the earth at the end of the second day is still covered with water. The water might have been only six inches deep over Mount Everest, but it still is covered (See Figure 5).

CHAPTER 3

Day 3

> And God said, "Let the waters under the heaven
> be gathered together unto one place, and let the
> dry land appear:" and it was so." (Genesis 1:9)

This is the first appearance of dry land on the face of the earth. Scientists would tell us that dry land had been on earth for millions of years and that dinosaurs roamed the earth up until sixty million years ago when they became extinct. The Bible tells us otherwise.

The question is, where did all that water go that covered the mountains? The sphere of ice encapsulating the earth would still be up there at about one hundred thousand feet or approximately eighteen to twenty miles. The rest of the water except for the water in the fresh water seas went into the lower caverns in the earth.

> Or who shut up the sea with doors, when it burst
> forth and issued from the womb; when I made the
> clouds its garment, and thick darkness its swad-
> dling band; when I fixed My limit for it, and set
> bars and doors; when I said, This far you may

come, but no further, and hear your proud waves must stop! (Job 38:8–11 (NKJV))

Here God is telling Job that He is the one who set the boundaries for the water. Notice that the water is kept in a womb-like cavern with doors set to keep it in place. In other words, the earth at creation did not look like the earth you and I live on today. It did not have seventy-five percent of the earth's surface covered with water. It had small seas of fresh water to provide water for humans and animals, but most of the water was held in caverns in the lower parts of the earth and, of course, the water in frozen form in the sphere surrounding the earth. The earth today is under the curse and wobbles through space like a drunken sailor.

Psalm 33:7 (NKJV) tells us that God stored the water in storehouses:

He gathers the waters of the sea together as a heap [the Septuagint, Targum, and Vulgate read "in a vessel"]; He lays up the deep in storehouses.

These verses suggest that God stored the waters in caverns (a womb) or containers (vessels) and that these were located below the surface of the earth. Even today you can walk up a mountain and find springs of water coming out and running down in the form of creeks and rivers. How can this be? Water is stored below the surface of the earth and is delivered to the surface as a result of pressure forcing the waters to the surface. This provides us with fresh drinking water from springs.

Another indication is shown in Genesis 2:4–6 where God created the earth and the heavens, and there were no plants, trees, grass, or no living things, for God had not caused it to rain on the earth. And there was no man to till the ground, for God had not created him at this time. Then the Bible states:

[B]ut a mist went up from the earth and watered the whole face of the ground. (Genesis 2:6
(NKJV))

This makes it clear that there was no rain and water for the
vegetation came up from below the ground to nourish the plants.

Recently I watched a documentary on television entitled *The
Water Age*, where they have found a large body of water under
the nation of Brazil the size of England, France, and Spain com-
bined. They estimate there is enough water there to provide one
hundred liters of water every day for every person on earth for
two hundred years.

They further estimate water being discovered below ground
and even under the ocean bed could provide a thousand times all
the water supplied by all the lakes and rivers in the earth. They
have rigs sitting on the floor of the ocean presently drilling for
water just like they drill for oil.

Iceland is another example of a water source trapped below
the surface. They can drill down two thousand meters and get
hot water (300 degrees centigrade) coming to the surface in the
form of steam, which they use to generate electricity, heat everyone's home, and now they are moving to totally eliminate the use
of fossil fuels. They are experimenting with hydrogen-powered
buses, which give off water as a by-product, thus eliminating
pollution.

Yes, God knew what He was doing when He created the earth
and stored all that water in the bowels of the earth.

And God called the dry land Earth, and the gath-
ering together of the waters He called seas. (Genesis 1:10 (NKJV))

The seas spoken of here are small fresh water seas located
around the earth to provide drinking water. They also could

mean underground seas, and we know there are lakes and seas of water below the earth's surface like the one they discovered in Brazil.

The Green Earth

And God said, "Let the earth bring forth grass, the herb yielding seed, and the fruit tree yielding fruit after his kind, whose seed is in itself, upon the earth: and it was so." (Genesis 1:11)

This is the first vegetation that appeared on the earth at God's command. The whole earth is now a planet covered with green vegetation. We must not think of the earth as we see it today with three quarters of the surface covered with water. The pictures we have seen of the earth as viewed from outer space looks beautiful with its blue oceans, brownish-tan land masses, and white cloud covers, but the earth you and I see today is under the curse and is not anything like the original creation. The earth at this time in the creation process was a green earth, and all this vegetation will fulfill God's intended purpose in the future.

Just think for a minute of all the oceans being dry land with great canyons and high mountain peaks and all covered in rich vegetation to feed a huge population like the earth has never seen since before the flood.

The Bible tells us from Adam to Noah's flood was 1,654 years. Humans and beasts all had a diet of vegetation. Animals did not kill animals, and humans did not kill animals for food; therefore, the population naturally increased exponentially. There are charts available on the Internet that show the population at nine billion to seventeen billion people, not counting animals. All need to be fed daily, and that's why God made the original earth a green earth before the curse and before the flood.

> And the earth brought forth grass, and herb yield-
> ing seed after his kind, and the tree yielding fruit,
> whose seed was in itself, after his kind: and God
> saw that it was good. (Genesis 1:12)

Verse 12 is another example of a descriptive verse following what God spoke into existence in verse 11. The grass came forth, and the trees grew and gave their fruit from the seed within them. Notice also that God has outsmarted the evolutionist He knew would come along centuries later and say that all this happened over millions of years slowly evolving into what are now fruit trees. God said here in verse 12 for the first time that the grass and the trees came forth "after their kind," meaning grass does not evolve into trees or trees into grass, but they reproduce after their kind. When we get to animals (and humans), we will see the same statement from God Himself that they will reproduce after their own kind.

Remember, at this point in time of the creation week, there are no stars, no sun, and no moon set in their place in the universe. The light in the universe at this time was produced by God Himself (Jesus); He is the light.

The grass and the trees need the life-giving sunlight to survive. It is a proven fact that grass cannot survive without sunlight for more than twenty-eight days. That's another reason why I believe a creation day was a twenty-four-hour day and not a thousand years or millions of years that some like to say. If the creation day was a thousand years long, all the vegetation and fruit trees God just created would be dead.

After God established the green earth, that ended the third creation day.

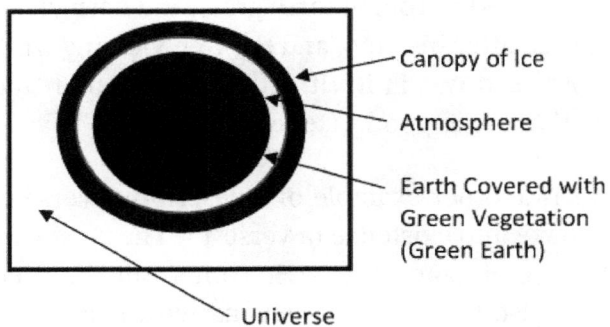

Fig. 6. The green earth (Genesis 1:12).

CHAPTER 4

Day 4

And God said, Let there be lights in the firmament of the heaven to divide the day from the
night; and let them be for signs, and for seasons,
and for days, and years: And let them be for lights
in the firmament of the heaven to give light upon
the earth: and it was so. (Genesis 1:14–15)

God did not wait long at all to set in place the life-giving
sphere of the sun that nourishes the grass and trees,
giving light to all on the earth, and keeps us warm from
the cold temperature of outer space. Did you know that if the
sun did not shine, earth would become a frozen ice ball with
no living plants, animals, or humans? God knew just what was
required to make a perfect creation. Even the earth's distance
from the sun is critical. If the earth were closer, the temperatures would soar and would not support human life. The same
is true if the earth were farther away from the sun than it presently is, we would freeze from colder temperatures and longer
seasons. How great and wonderful is our God.

Notice that verse 15 gives the purpose for creating the sun,
moon, and stars.

> And God made two great lights; the greater light
> to rule the day, and the lesser light to rule the
> night; He made the stars also. (Genesis 1:16–17)

In these two verses, we have the descriptive verse adding more information to what happened in verses 14 and 15. God made the sun, the greater light; the moon, which is the lesser light; then in just five words it says that "He made the stars also." What a wonderful process of creation we have here. We have the sun giving life and warmth for the day and the warm glow of the moon for the night. And all the billions and billions of stars set in precise places in space. He placed planets with such precise orbits you can set your watch by them and establish a calendar for seasons and years. God is the greatest mathematician who ever existed.

Some of the stars are in a fixed position in relation to the earth, which allows the scientists to measure and calculate the position of the earth and planets in our solar system. Scientists can calculate where the earth was in relation to the fixed stars years ago and also where the earth and planets will be years in the future. God established the precise movement of the planets, and he established their mathematics. Man just discovered how to calculate the position of the planets in the sixteenth and seventeenth centuries.

How wonderful and magnificent is our God.

> And to rule over the day and over the night, and to
> divide the light from the darkness; and God saw
> that it was good. (Genesis 1:18)

God did not have to go back and change what He had just created. Humans have to make changes to improve what they make because what they make is not perfect, but God's original creation was perfect, and He so much as said so when He said, "It is good."

This ended the fourth day of creation with all types of vegetation receiving nourishment from the sun.

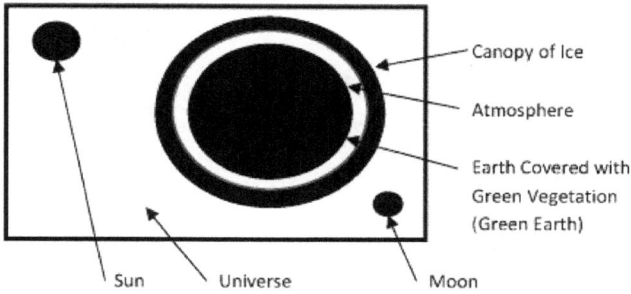

Fig. 7. The sun, moon, and stars created (Genesis 1:16–17).

CHAPTER 5

Day 5

And God said, Let the waters bring forth abundantly the moving creature that hath life, and fowl that may fly above the earth in the open firmament of heaven. (Genesis 1:20)

On this day, God created living creatures to inhabit the earth. He started by creating all sorts of living creatures that would live in water, then He created the birds that would fly in the open space of the First heaven. The open space of the First heaven is the space between the earth and the ice canopy, approximately eighteen to twenty miles up in the atmosphere.

Did this act of creation include dinosaurs? I believe it did. Remember, under two atmospheres of pressure animals could grow much larger than they do today. In fact, Job 40 alludes to this type of creature living on the earth.

Job 40:15–18 describes a large land animal like none we see living today. Job must have seen them, otherwise he would not have known what God was talking about when He described the animals tail. Dinosaurs lived after the six days of creation and evidently were alive during Job's testing.

> Look now at the behemoth, which I made along
> with you [no evolution here]; He eats grass like
> an ox. See now, his strength is in his hips, and his
> power is in his stomach muscles. He moves his tail
> like a cedar; The sinews of his thighs are tightly
> knit. His bones are like beams of bronze, His ribs
> like bars of iron. (Job 40:15–18 (NKJV))

Some have tried to say this animal was a hippopotamus. How
ridiculous is that. Have you ever seen a hippo with a tail as large
as a cedar tree? They have a very short, puny tail. What is described here is a dinosaur, and they coexisted with humans and
other animals before the flood as a vegetarian, the same as the
other animals.

At this stage of the creation process, we have all the dinosaurs,
flying creatures, and sea creatures that the scientists claim died
out sixty million years ago. They lived alongside Adam, and neither feared for their lives. Adam named all of the animals. I believe they walked right up to him and coexisted in peace with
each other. Isaiah 11:6–8 tells us that the animal kingdom is going to change where they will no longer be flesh-eating creatures
as they are today but will return to their pre-flood makeup. They
will become vegetarian once again, and humans can coexist with
them just like Adam did.

> So God created great sea creatures and every
> living thing that moves, with which the waters
> abounded, according to their kind, and every
> winged bird according to its kind. And God saw
> that it was good. (Genesis 1:21 (NKJV))

Here again we have verse 21 following verse 20, with verse
21 being descriptive of what God performed as a creative act.
The creatures reproduced "after their kind." God knew from the

beginning of the world that one day there would be people who would say that God had nothing to do with creation. It all happened with the big bang, and the living creatures evolved from a one-celled blob living in some pond full of muck and goo. Did you notice how specific God was about Him being the creator when He was talking with Job?

> Look now at the behemoth, which I made along with you. (Job 40:15)

> In the beginning was the Word, and the Word was with God, and the Word was God. The same was in the beginning with God. All things were made by Him; and without Him was not any thing made that was made. (John 1:1–3)

God takes ownership of creation when He made that statement to Job, and John reiterates Jesus as the creator. Also, how could Job look at the behemoth if it ceased to exist sixty million years ago? God also states in Isaiah 45:12 that He and He alone is the creator. He states, "I have made the earth and created man on it" (Isaiah 45:12). It doesn't matter what the scientists say. It doesn't matter what the atheists say. God has the final word on truth. You see, if God does not speak the truth, then He would no longer be God. To finish this verse, just remember the verse following a creative verse, a verse where God performed a creative act, describes what happened in that creative act. It adds detail.

> And God blessed them, saying, "Be fruitful, and multiply, and fill the waters in the seas, and let fowl multiply in the earth." (Genesis 1:22)

God was offering a blessing to all the creatures He just created and was instructing them to multiply and fill the earth and the seas with their offspring. This verse gives additional details concerning verse 20, where God created the creatures in the first place. With this creative act, the fifth day of creation ended.

CHAPTER 6

Day 6

And God said, "Let the earth bring forth the living creature after his kind, cattle and creeping thing, and beast of the earth, after his kind: and it was so." (Genesis 1:24)

God was populating the earth with all kinds of living creatures. He further states that they would reproduce after their own kind. Sorry evolutionists, but cattle produce cattle; horses produce horses; dogs produce dogs; and so forth. Your bankrupt theory presently taught to our children in schools across America and the world is just that, a bankrupt, unproven theory that lacks operational scientific proof. In fact, every time an archeologist comes up with another bone that supposedly proves evolution to be true, it turns out, after further investigation, to be another falsehood and dead end.

After God said for the creatures to come forth, the Bible says, "[A]nd it was so." God said it, and it was so. Scientists and archeologists can't accept that. They now have a godless theory they have stood on for so long and to such a degree that they will not admit they were wrong. It's like the child who climbed out on the limb of a tree and when it began to move and shake like it would break any moment, the child froze and could not get off the limb.

Neither can the scientists. They have left behind the science of honest investigation establishing empirical evidence to prove their theories to be true, but instead they expect us to accept what they say as fact without proof. So, they go on teaching our children lies and unproven theories through the textbooks. The educators and scientists criticize the faith community for believing what the Bible says by faith, yet it takes the same measure of faith and even more to believe in their godless, unproven theory of evolution. They don't have God's Word to back them up. They just pull their theory out of the air and think you should accept it because they said so. Well, good science requires empirical evidence to prove a theory, and we don't have to accept it until they do. Do you think the people writing and selling the school textbooks would correct the errors when exposed? Not in your wildest dreams. The people writing your child's school books will not revise them to present the truth. They will continue to print the lies. It is up to the parents of children, first of all, and the church, secondly, to instruct the children under their care of the truth of the Word of God. If we fail to do that, our children will be taught by misguided educators.

> And God made the beast of the earth after his kind, and cattle after their kind, everything that creepeth upon the earth after his kind: and God saw that it was good. (Genesis 1:25 (NKJV))"

This verse is descriptive of verse 24, where the creatures were created. Remember the pattern—a creative act is followed by a verse that is descriptive of the creative act. It also shows that the creeping things were created at this time, and all reproduced after their kind. God looked on what He had created and said that "it was good."

> Then God said, Let us make man in our own im-
> age, after our likeness: and let them have domin-
> ion over the fish of the sea, and over the fowl of
> the air, and over the cattle, and over all the earth,
> and over every creeping thing that creepeth upon
> the earth. (Genesis 1:26)

God then turned to His greatest of all creations, man. You see, man was created in God's image, which is different from all the other creatures He created.

God is a three-part being consisting of the Father, the Son, and the Holy Spirit. God is not three separate persons but one God with three separate entities. When God created the heavens and the earth as mentioned in Genesis 1, that included Jesus and the Holy Spirit. Genesis 1:2 states that the Holy Spirit hovered over the waters. John 1:1–3 states:

> In the beginning was the Word, and the Word was
> with God, and the Word was God. The same was
> in the beginning with God. All things were made
> by Him; and without Him was not anything made
> that was made.

Now isn't that plain? God made everything that was made, and it was done by the Word (Jesus Christ) who was with God and the Holy Spirit. They are always together; they are always in agreement; and they are all the same God, the three in one. Jesus, when He took on the body of man and walked on this earth, was doing the will of the Father. When Jesus left the earth to go be with the Father in heaven, He sent the Holy Spirit to comfort us. John 10:30 states, "I and My Father are one." First John 5:7 also confirms the oneness of the Trinity, "For there are three that bear witness in heaven: The Father, the Word, and the Holy Spirit; and these three are one."

So, in Genesis 1:26, we have God the Father, God the Son (the Word), and God the Holy Spirit included in one person, God. They were about to create a man made in three parts: body, soul, and spirit. Humans are made as a trinity just like God is. Mankind was created with a body, a soul, and a spirit. The human soul has a will, intuition, knowledge, and understanding. Humans also have a spirit, which is capable of communicating with God through the Holy Spirit.

The animals God created are not made this way. They have instincts to guide them. Humans and animals both die and their bodies return to the earth, but when humans die, their spirit goes to be with the Lord, if they are Christians. It's not so with the animals—their spirits go down to the earth according to Ecclesiastes 3:19–21 (NKJV):

> For what happens to the sons of men also happens to animals; one thing befalls them: as one dies, so dies the other. Surely, they all have one breath; man has no advantage over animals, for all is vanity. All go to one place: all are from the dust, and all return to dust. Who knows the spirit of the sons of men, which goes upward, and the spirit of the animal, which goes down to the earth.

God gave Man authority over all the earth. He gave Man dominion over all the animals and over all the earth. It's like the husbandman who owned a vineyard who put a manager over it to prune it and care for it. The husbandman expected to receive a harvest from this arrangement. God, by putting Man over the earth, expected Man to obey Him, to nurture, and to take care of the whole earth and all that lived therein. The result would be offspring who loved and worshipped the creator. We know this was messed up when Adam and Eve sinned against God and brought on the curse and the fall of all mankind. We have been suffering under the curse ever since. Just look around the earth today; you are not looking at an earth the way God created it. God created a perfect world, a paradise. The earth groans under the curse and longs for God to bring it back to the original created state, which He will do one day.

> So God created man in His own image, in the image of God created he him; male and female created he them. (Genesis 1:27)

Verse 27 reemphasizes what God did in verse 26. Man was created in God's image. He created Adam first, and we don't know how long after Adam was created that He made Eve from one of Adam's ribs. We know this because Adam had the job of naming all the animals, and as he watched and saw them reproducing with their mates, he was lonely for a mate himself. That's when God made Eve. Eve must have been a beautiful woman because God himself made all her features appealing to Adam. Today we can see many beautiful women, but I think they must pale in comparison with Eve.

> And God blessed them, and God said unto them, "Be fruitful, and multiply, and replenish (*fill*) the earth, and subdue it: and have dominion over the fish of the sea, over the fowl of the air, and over every living thing that moveth upon the earth." (Genesis 1:28)

First, notice that Adam and Eve received a blessing from God, then instruction to become fruitful by reproducing offspring to fill the earth. God reiterated man's God-given authority over all living creatures on the earth, in the waters, and in the air.

Man (Adam) is the federal head over the human race with dominion over all living creatures. God gave man much power and authority.

Man's relation with the animal world is one of coexistence and respect. The animals before the flood were peaceful and did not attack and kill one another or humans. Humans also did not kill the animals. They had no need to do so. mankind and animals alike were vegetarian as the next two verses verify.

> And God said, "Behold, I have given you every herb bearing seed, which is upon the face of all the earth, and every tree, in the which is the fruit of a tree yielding seed; to you it shall be for meat. And to every beast of the earth, to every fowl of the air, and to everything that creepeth upon the earth, wherein there is life, I have given every green herb for meat:"; and it was so. (Genesis 1:29–30)

This ended the sixth day of creation.

Summary

Let's summarize what the earth looked like and the environment humans and animals lived in at the end of the six days of creation.

The earth was totally covered with green vegetation over an estimated ninety percent of the surface. It would have looked like a giant green planet viewed from outer space. There were fresh water seas, but not oceans like we see today. The water was stored in caverns below the surface of the earth and also in the sphere or canopy of ice that encapsulated the earth. Between the sphere of ice and the earth was a firmament or atmosphere as described in Genesis 1:6. This is the atmosphere we know today.

The sphere of ice could have been eighteen to twenty miles up in the sky. This sphere of ice protected the earth from harmful rays emitted from the sun and created a pressurized atmosphere of two atmospheres or about 32 psi. This meant that humans and animals took in more oxygen with every breath, making them healthy and strong and giving them a longer life. This also could account for the fact that humans up until the flood enjoyed long life with vitality. God's original plan was for Adam and Eve to have eternal life on the planet, but this was interrupted when they sinned in the garden of Eden.

I call the earth at this stage "the green earth" because that's what it would look like from outer space. As I have said several times, humans and animals coexisted in harmony. They did not kill each other, and I believe Adam could walk right up to an animal we would consider dangerous today and pet it. Adam nor the animals feared one another. They were just like pets. Why would Eve let a snake get close to her in the garden of Eden unless she had no fear of it?

At this point, the earth had a food supply of vegetation, as all creatures were vegetarians. There were creatures and fish in the seas and fowls in the atmosphere. The temperature was a constant 72 degrees Fahrenheit. God had made provision for all their needs.

CHAPTER 7

Day 7

Thus the heavens and the earth were finished, and all the host of them. (Genesis 2:1)

This is a short sentence, but it is loaded with the creative actions of our Creator and God. God finished creating the heavens. There are three heavens mentioned in the Bible. The first heaven is the atmosphere just above the earth where the birds and planes fly. Genesis 1:20 tells us that birds fly in this firmament: "[A]nd God said, let the waters bring forth abundantly the moving creature that hath life, and the fowl that may fly above the earth in the open firmament of heaven." The firmament or first heaven contains the oxygen we breathe. God made provision for living creatures to have life-sustaining oxygen to breathe, otherwise we would be dead in minutes. It is first mentioned in Genesis 1:6 where God said, "Let there be a firmament in the midst of the waters, and let it divide the waters from the waters." This occurred on the second day of creation.

When God spoke this, the earth was entirely covered with water, so He divided the water so that some of it went up in the sky, forming the sphere of ice that encased the earth. At this point, there was still enough water on the face of the earth to cover the mountains. We know this because dry land did not appear until Genesis 1:9, or at the beginning of the third day of creation.

Next, we see that God created a second heaven where the sun, moon, and stars reside.

> On the fourth day of creation God said "Let there be lights in the firmament of the heaven to divide the day from the night. (Genesis 1:14) And God made two great lights; the greater light to rule the day, and the lesser light to rule the night: He made the stars also." (Genesis 1:16)

This second heaven is known to us as outer space. It contains no oxygen and is dark as a coal mine except for the light emitted by the stars and the sun(s) located there. God provided the sun and the moon for humankind to survive on the earth. Without the light and heat radiating from the sun, life on earth would cease to exist. The astronauts must wear special suits when they travel into the second heaven so they can breathe. The second heaven is a vacuum, meaning an object acted upon by an outside force will travel in a straight line until acted upon by another force. There is no gravity like we have on earth. Astronauts must be tethered to their space vehicle to keep from flying away into outer space. The second heaven is known to us as the universe or outer space.

The third heaven is where God resides. It is where his throne room exists and most likely is light-years from earth, yet Jesus traveled from earth to the third heaven and back to earth in a very short period of time (the same day). We read of this in John 20:15–17, where Mary Magdalene confronted Jesus after he had risen from the grave. She thought he was the gardener and asked where he had placed the body of Jesus, but when Jesus spoke to her, she recognized His voice and knew it was Jesus. She evidently moved toward him to grab him and hug him, but He told her not to touch Him, for He had not yet ascended to his Father in heaven. Jesus, in these verses, was telling Mary that He must ascend to heaven to present His shed blood as the perfect sacrifice for mankind's sins. He must go into the temple located in heaven, enter the holy of holies, and place His blood on the mercy seat. God the Father saw that it was a perfect and acceptable sacrifice, which took care of the sin problem. Jesus then traveled back to earth in an instant (by translation) to be with the disciples that evening. Jesus ate with them, showing that even with His resurrected body that can pass through solid doors, He was able to eat fish just as before. Jesus let doubting Thomas touch the wounds in His hands and side to prove that it was He who was crucified and lives.

> And On the seventh day God ended His work which He had made; and He rested on the seventh day from all the work which He had made. (Genesis 2:2)

Now, do you think God was tired from all this exertion of creating the universe and all that was in it? No! God does not get tired like we do. However, God knew we needed an example or we most likely would kill ourselves with endless work and no rest. Humans, when they get so busy with things of this world, whether work or play, tend to forget God. God took the time to rest as an example of what we should do each week. More than that, God desires to have fellowship and communion with us because He loves us so much. God, therefore, set aside one day out of the week whereby we might commune with Him and worship Him. God wants us to have communion with Him daily, but the seventh day is special. He did that with Adam at the beginning when He walked in the garden each evening and they talked. God wants us to talk to Him and enjoy His fellowship. Far too many Christians fail to talk much to God, and they leave Him waiting.

Let's consider how important God considers the sabbath, the day of rest. Leviticus 19:3 states, "Ye shall fear every man, his mother and his father, and keep My Sabbaths: I am the LORD your God." Here God puts keeping His Sabbaths on the same level as honoring your mother and father.

In Leviticus 25:1–5, God lays down the requirements for keeping the Sabbath in the land where he says:

> And the LORD spoke unto Moses in Mount Sinai, saying, "Speak unto the children of Israel, and say unto them, When ye come into the land which I give you, then shall the land keep a sabbath unto the LORD. Six years thou shalt sow thy field, and six years thou shalt prune thy vineyard, and gather in the fruit thereof; but in the seventh year shall be a sabbath of rest unto the land, a sabbath for the LORD: thou shalt neither sow Thy field, nor prune thy vineyard. That which groweth of its own accord of thy harvest thou shalt not reap, neither gather the grapes of thy vine undressed, for it is a year of rest unto the land."

God made provision for them during the sixth year by providing a bumper crop that would last three years according to Leviticus 25:20–21.

Now, historically, here's what happened. King Saul, the first king of Israel became king around 1096 BC. King David and king Solomon following until the kingdom split into the Northern kingdom of Israel and the Southern kingdom of Judah. From king Solomon there were eighteen kings up to an including King Eliakim (renamed Jehoiakim). King Eliakim was renamed by the king of Egypt who had just conquered Jerusalem (2 Chronicles 36:4). Jehoiakim was reigning in 606 BC, when king Nebchadnezzar conquered Judah and took Daniel and his friends captivity in Babylon. There were four hundred ninety years where the nation of Judah did not observe the Sabbath of the Lord. Now God does not set down requirements for mankind, then let man go about disobeying them without recourse. So, in Jeremiah 25:11, it states Judah will be in captivity for seventy years. Why seventy years? Four hundred ninety years of not observing the Lord's Sabbaths (one for each seven years) divided by seven equals seventy years of captivity in Babylon.

As stated above, the Lord's Sabbath was established on the seventh day of creation, and God expected man to observe it. God will get His Sabbaths for the land even to the extent of allowing a foreign nation to bring Israel and Judah into submission by removing them from their land.

We have gone through the seven days of creation using the Scriptures and just taking seriously what the Word of God says. God created a perfect world and set Adam and Eve in a beautiful garden where they could have enjoyed eternal life had they not failed God and His commands.

Notice that we did not add a gap between verses 1 and 2 so there would be billions of years of evolution. To believe in evolution, you must take away from God His power and creativity. You are in effect saying the earth and all the creatures had to come into being by some natural event or process without God. By believing that, you now have a godless religion called evolution. Those believing in the big bang theory believe the universe came into being not by God's creative ability and power but by an explosion of some matter that mysteriously appeared in outer space. They can't explain where the matter came from or what it was. Their view of the universe and its beginning does not start with earth but with matter in outer space. They view the earth as no more important than any other planet. That might be the reason why space scientists today are looking for another planet like earth that can support life. They want to go there and set up a civilization to inhabit the new planet. God in His Word starts with the earth and ends with the earth. They will never find a planet like the earth. They believe after billions of years of evolution, humans came into existence from a one-celled creature that evolved into a fish, a toad, a monkey, and finally into you. Their view is that humans are always moving to a higher form, a better human, but Scripture shows us that humans are on a downward tract of degradation. Humans are not getting better, but instead are getting farther from God. God is left out completely because they think it is all a natural process. Sadly, this lie is being taught in our schools today as "proven truth" when in fact it is not a truth but an outright lie from the pit of hell.

This lie is causing children to believe their parents, who believe in the Bible's version of creation, are ignorant and wrong, and it is a cause for many of our young people today leaving our churches.

Evolution is one of the tools Satan is using to try to tear down the foundation of the Bible. You see, if he can destroy our belief in the creation (page 1 of the Bible) as presented in the Bible, he can destroy the need for a Savior. If there is no need for a Savior, then Jesus was not the Savior, and it all falls apart. Also, if Jesus was not the Savior, then our faith is in vain, and Jesus would be a fool for going to the cross for something He knew was untrue. We know however, Jesus was God incarnate who came to earth as the Christ to pay the sin debt against each of us and to give us victory over death, hell, and the grave. Romans 3:23 states, "For all have sinned and come short of the glory of God."

I implore you to not allow the schools, your friends, or anyone to change you from believing the Bible's version of creation. Even churches today are being deceived to believe the lie. Yes! It seems they are quick to compromise with the world and disregard what God says in His Word.

CHAPTER 8

Age of the Earth

There has been much discussion about how old the earth is. The age of the earth is an important subject because it either supports evolution and the godless theories associated with it or it supports the Bible and what God says in His Word. The age of the earth, therefore, is also foundational to the truth of the Bible (God's Word). Years ago, people would buy and sell property on a handshake. Why? Because a person's word was their bond. In other words, a person's word meant something. You could take it to the bank. Not so today. People have lost the importance of telling the truth and standing behind what they say or promise. Today you need to have a written contract drawn up by an attorney, one that you can hold a person to keeping what that person promised through the law. This shows the sad state mankind is in.

Some of the unproven theories scientists and educators are espousing today are evolution and the big bang theory—both which are godless. Remember, evolution requires billions and billions of years for the theory to be considered workable. If the earth is only a few thousand years old as the Bible shows, then evolution won't work as we would see evidence of the different stages of transformation of humans and animals. If the theory of evolution were true, we could go to the zoo and see animals at various stages of transformation, even half animal and half human, but we don't because it is a fake and false theory unproven by empirical evidence. Empirical evidence is what the people in the science community are supposed to obtain to prove a theory to be true, otherwise it is declared false. We who study God's Word know this is a theory without basis and truth. It is an outright lie accepted by many today and taught in our public school system. So, what we need to do is see what God has to say about the age of the earth. Remember this: God is all-knowing, meaning He knows the beginning from the end, so He knew there would be a problem with false information from the scientists claiming evolution and the big bang theories to be true and that God was not part of the process. These theories are used by Satan to confuse humanity's view of God. God in His wisdom put in the Scriptures a genealogical lineage record of evidence from the beginning to the end. Humans can dispute it all they want, but God said it and it is true.

In order to study God's record, we will look at the recorded genealogies in the Bible to start with. I know genealogies are not much fun to read, but if you will stick with me on this journey, we will get to our destination quickly. I remember as a young boy who had just accepted Jesus as my Savior wanting to read the Bible. I used my parents' huge family Bible to start with and soon began to read the genealogies in Genesis. Boy, was that hard to read. The names were hard to pronounce as well. Later in life as I studied the Word more, I was drawn back to the genealogies where as a draftsman, I began to make a scaled drawing of the lifelines of the genealogies. I would lay it down for several years and pick it up again, but finally when I became a Sunday school teacher, I mapped out the genealogies and other verses showing the age of the earth from God's Word.

Let's start with Adam, who God created on the sixth day of creation, which was a twenty-four-hour day (Genesis 1:26–27; 2:7–25). We will take the year a person is born, or in the case of

Adam, when he was created, and add the years until his son in the lineage of Christ Jesus is born, thus forming an unbroken chain through history. In Genesis 5:3–32, we find Adam lived to be nine hundred thirty years old; but the important thing is that he lived one hundred thirty years before Seth was born. Seth lived one hundred five years before Enos was born. Enos lived ninety years before Cainan was born. Cainan lived seventy years before Mahalaleel was born. Mahalaleel lived sixty-five years before Jared was born. Jared lived one hundred sixty-two years before Enoch was born. Enoch lived sixty-five years before Methuselah was born. Methuselah lived eighty-seven years before Lamech was born. Lamech lived one hundred eighty-two years before Noah was born. Noah lived five hundred years before Shem was born. It should be noted here that Noah lived three hundred fifty years after the flood, which occurred 1,654 years after creation. Noah lived a total of nine hundred fifty years. Genesis 11:10 lists Shem living one hundred years before Arphaxad was born, which occurred two years after the flood. That means that Shem was ninety-eight years old at the time of the flood. With this information, we can pinpoint the flood occurring 1,654 years after Adam was created, or after the sixth day of creation. Arphaxad lived thirty-five years before Salah was born. Salah lived thirty years before Eber was born. Eber lived thirty-four years before Peleg was born. Peleg lived thirty years before Reu was born. Reu lived thirty-two years before Serug was born. Serug lived thirty years before Nahor was born. Nahor lived twenty-nine years before Terah was born. Terah lived seventy years before Abram was born. Do you see how God in His Word established an unbroken chain of births so we could calculate the age of the earth even though scientists want to tell us the earth is billions of years old and evolution teachers want us to believe we evolved from a one-celled ameba.

Now add up all the years before each birth took place and you get 1,946 years from Adam to Abram's birth. Now we must deal with the sojourn of Israel over a period of four hundred or four hundred-thirty years. Which is correct? Genesis 12:4–5 tells us that Abram was seventy-five years old when he left the town of Haran for the land of Canaan. Exodus 12:40–41 tells us that the children of Israel sojourned in Egypt and Canaan for four- hundred-thirty years and that they left Egypt exactly on the same day four-hundred-thirty years later. (Note: the KJV of the Bible states that Israel sojourned in Egypt only, whereas the Septuagint states the sojourn took place in Canaan and Egypt for four hundred-thirty years.) The Septuagint is the earliest Greek translation of the Hebrew Scriptures from the original Hebrew. Galatians 3:16–17 tells us that the law was given four hundred-thirty years from the time God promised Abraham a son (Isaac) until the Israelites left Egypt. First, notice Abram was seventy-five years old when God told him to leave Haran (Genesis 12:4).

In Genesis 16:3, we find that Abram got Hagar, Sari's maidservant, pregnant (by Sari's permission) and Ishmael was born when Abram was eighty-six years old. In Genesis 17:5, when Abram was ninety-nine years old, God changed his name to Abraham; then in verse 8, God gives Abraham and his descendants the land of Canaan as an everlasting possession. Genesis 15:18–21 describes the length and breadth of the land grant God made to Abram. It states,

> "In the same day the Lord made a covenant with Abram, saying, 'Unto thy seed (*descendants*) have I given this land, from the river of Egypt unto the great river, the river Euphrates:, The Kenites, and the Kenezzites, and the Kadmonites, And the Hittites, and the Perizzites, and the Rephaims, And the Amorites, and the Canannites, and the Girgashites, and the Jesbusites.'"

This is a description of all the people whose land God gave to Abram for an inheritance. Genesis 17:7–8 reiterates the covenant God made with Abram,

> "And I will establish My covenant between Me and thee and thy seed after thee in their generations for an everlasting covenant, to be a God unto thee and to thy seed after thee. Also, I give unto thee and to thy seed after thee, the land wherein thou art a stranger, all the land of Canaan, for an everlasting possession; and I will be their God."

That shows that the Palestinians today are trespassing on Jewish land, as are the people of Jordan, Lebanon, and Syria.

Genesis 17:17–19 shows us that Abraham was ninety-nine years old when God told him he would have a son called Isaac. In Genesis 21:8–9, when Isaac was five years old and Ishmael was nineteen years old, Isaac was being weaned, and Ishmael mocked him. This upset Sarah so much that she told Abraham that Hagar and Ishmael had to go. This was the beginning of the persecution of Abraham's offspring, which was contrary to God's perfect plan for Abraham. Exodus 12:40-41 shows us a four-hundred-thirty year period of time of sojourning in the land of Canaan and Egypt starting with Abraham leaving Haran at age seventy-five. Twenty-five years later Isaac is born and he is weaned at age five. This makes Abraham one hundred and five years old when Isaac is weaned and is thirty years after Abraham left Haran. When Isaac was weaned this started the clock ticking on the four hundred years remaining of the four hundred and thirty years mentioned in Exodus 12:40-41, until the children of Israel left Egypt. This persecution is an example of what happens when we get ahead of God and try to help Him with His plan. It happens in our lives as well, and there is always a price to pay. The Jews have been paying a price of persecution since Ishmael was born.

This mocking incident is important because as I said, it starts the clock ticking on the four hundred years that Abraham and his descendants sojourned in Canaan and Egypt. The four hundred thirty years God mentioned started when Abraham left Haran and entered Canaan. Using this information, we add seventy-five years from Abraham's birth until he left Haran for Canaan, and he sojourned there twenty-five years when Isaac was born (Ishmael was fourteen years old when Isaac born). When Ishmael was nineteen years old, he mocked Isaac at the time of his weaning at age five. Abraham has sojourned in Canaan thirty years by this time, and the mocking incident was the beginning of the persecution of Abraham's descendants for four hundred years. So, we have 1,946 years until Abram was born, plus one hundred to the birth of Isaac (the child of promise), plus five years to the weaning of Isaac, then four hundred years to the exodus for a total of 2,451 years from Adam to the exodus (1946 + 100 + 5 + 400 = 2,451 years).

Let's take another approach to connect our timeline of genealogies with history. Isaac was born when Abraham was one hundred years old (Genesis 21:5), then Jacob (Israel) and Esau were born when Isaac was sixty years old (Genesis 25:26). Genesis 47:9 shows us Israel (Jacob) was one hundred thirty years old when he stood before Pharaoh when he and his descendants moved to Egypt. This is going to be a key to connecting the genealogies with world history to get the age of the earth.

Now Genesis 41:46 tells us Joseph was thirty years old when he interpreted the king's dream and thereafter became the second in command in Egypt to prepare for the coming famine. The years of plenty were seven in number (Genesis 41:53), and Israel (Jacob) did not move to Egypt until the famine was two years into the seven-year famine (Genesis 45:6). This makes Joseph thirty-nine years old when his father came to Egypt (30 + 7 + 2 = 39). That also means Joseph ruled in Egypt another seventy-one years since he died at age one hundred ten (110 - 39 = 71).

Geneologies from Adam to Jacob

Name	Years to Birth of First Son	Years Lived	Years counting Age of Earth	Years BC	Years from Adam	Scripture
Adam	130	930	130	3947	0	Genesis 5:3-32
Seth	105	912	235	3817	130	
Enos	90	905	325	3712	235	
Cainan	70	910	395	3622	325	
Mahalaleel	65	895	460	3552	395	
Jared	162	962	622	3487	460	
Enoch	65	365	687	3325	622	
Methuselah	187	969	874	3260	687	
Lamech	182	777	1056	3073	874	
Noah	500	950	1556	2891	1056	Genesis 5:32 & 9:29
Shem	100	600	1656	2391	1556	Genesis 11:10-32
Arphaxad	35	438	1691	2291	1656	Gen. 11:10-13
Salah	30	433	1721	2256	1691	Gen. 11:14-15
Eber	34	464	1755	2226	1721	Gen. 11:16-17
Peleg	30	239	1785	2192	1755	Gen. 11:118-19
Reu	32	239	1817	2162	1785	Gen. 11:20-21
Serug	30	230	1847	2130	1817	Gen. 11:22-23
Nahor	29	148	1876	2100	1847	Gen. 11:24-25
Terah	70	205	1946	2071	1876	Gen. 11:26-32
Abraham	100	175	2046	2001	1946	Gen. 17:17 & 21:5 & 25:7
Isaac	60	180	2106	1901	2046	
Jacob		147	2106	1841	2106	

Fig. 8. Showing birth of the first child to determine lineage and age of earth.

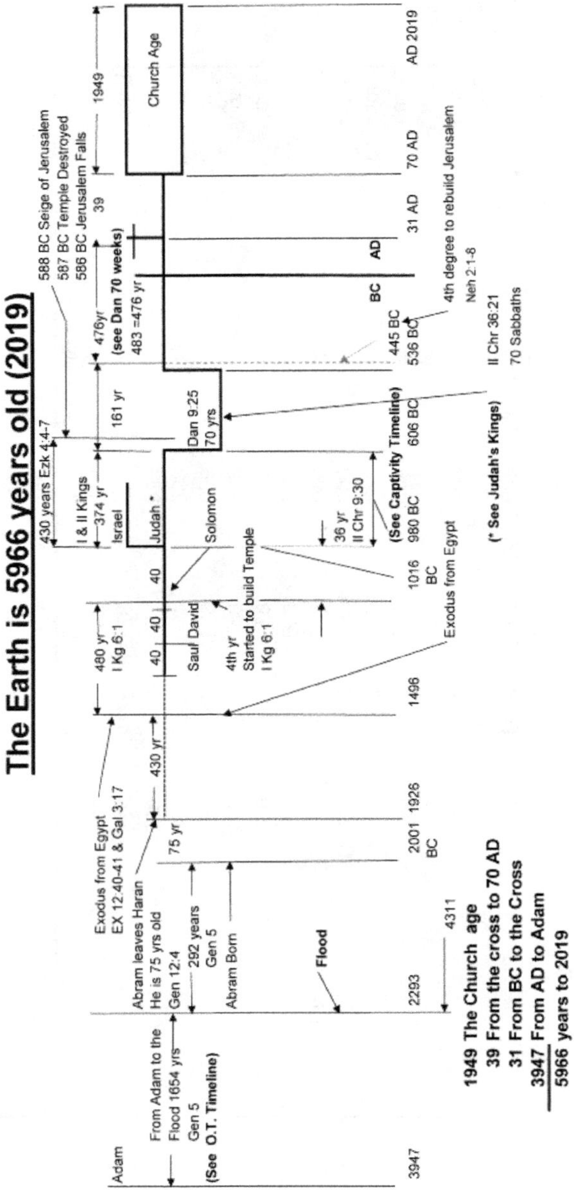

Fig. 9. Timeline from Adam to 2019.

The time Joseph ruled will be important later in our calculations. Now, if Israel (Jacob) was one hundred thirty years old when he stood before Pharaoh, and Joseph was thirty-nine years old, then Israel (Jacob) was ninety-one years old when Joseph was born (130 - 39 = 91).

We can take the time when Abraham left Haran when he was seventy-five years old (Genesis 12:4) and subtract that from Abraham's age when Isaac was born, and we see Abraham had been sojourning in Canaan twenty-five years before Isaac was born. We know according to Jewish tradition a child must be weaned by age five, and we know Ishmael mocked Isaac when he was weaned (Genesis 21:8–9); therefore, Abraham sojourned in Canaan thirty years when the persecution from Jacob's relation (Ishmael) started. The persecution would occur for another four hundred years ending in slavery in Egypt. Now add sixty years before Isaac had Jacob (Genesis 25:26), plus the one hundred thirty years when Jacob (Israel) moved his family to Egypt because the famine was in the land. We can add these times up and that will take us to the middle of the four hundred thirty years God said Abraham and his descendants would sojourn in Canaan and Egypt before they would come out free (Exodus 12:40; (25 + 60 + 130 = 215).

This shows Jacob entered Egypt exactly in the middle of the four hundred thirty years of sojourning in Canaan and Egypt mentioned in Exodus 12:40–41. There remains another two hundred fifteen years which includes the period of slavery in Egypt.

Let's look at the second half of the four hundred thirty years of sojourning and slavery, or the two hundred fifteen years in Egypt.

We showed earlier that Joseph ruled for seventy-one years in Egypt after Jacob entered the land of Egypt. Joseph lived to be one hundred ten years old. He was thirty years old when he stood before Pharaoh and interpreted his dream (Genesis 41:46). There were seven years of plenty followed by seven years of famine prophesied in the dream. Jacob did not enter Egypt until two years after the famine began, so we can add Joseph's age of thirty, plus seven years of plenty, plus two years of famine, and find that Joseph was thirty-nine years old when Jacob entered Egypt. Now, since Joseph lived one hundred ten years, we subtract thirty-nine years, and we find Joseph ruled in Egypt seventy-one years after Jacob entered Egypt (110 - 39 = 71 years).

Next, we know Moses was born eighty years before the exodus (Exodus 7:7). We know Moses was forty years old when he visited the children of Israel (Acts 7:23). He spent another forty years in the desert as a sheepherder with his father-in-law Jethro, thus making him eighty years old when God called him to lead the children of Israel out of Egypt (Acts 7:30 tells us forty years had passed in his desert experience).

If we take the last half of the sojourn in Egypt and subtract the seventy-one years Joseph ruled in Egypt after Jacob entered Egypt and subtract eighty years from Moses's birth until the Exodus, we have sixty-four years between the death of Joseph and the birth of Moses. The last forty years of Moses's life were spent leading the children of Israel around in the desert because God would not allow that generation go into the promised land because of their unbelief. Moses died at age one hundred twenty, and God buried him so no person would worship him. It should be noted here that the sixty-four years from the death of Joseph until Moses led the Israelites out of Egypt was the time of great enslavement. This was the time of hard labor making the bricks to build the cities in Egypt under hard taskmasters.

Let's compare the two paths we have laid out to get from the birth of Abram to the exodus.

Path 1:
- Abram left Haran at seventy-five years old.
- Abraham, Isaac, and Jacob sojourned in Canaan for two hundred fifteen years.

- The Israelites sojourned in Egypt for two hundred fifteen years.
- Total above equals 505 years + 1,946 years from Adam to Abram = 2,451 years.

Path 2:

- Abraham was one hundred years old at Isaac's birth.
- Isaac was sixty years old at Jacob's birth.
- Jacob (Israel) entered Egypt at age one hundred thirty.
- Joseph ruled in Egypt for seventy-one years (after Jacob came to Egypt).
- Joseph's death until Moses birth was a period of sixty-four years.
- Moses's birth until the exodus was a period of eighty years.
- Total above equals 505 years + 1,946 years from Adam to Abram = 2,451 years.

Next, we take the years calculated above and begin to connect to world history as follows:

If we take 2,451 years and add four hundred eighty years from the exodus until King Solomon's temple was dedicated in the fourth year of King Solomon's reign (1 Kings 6:1), plus thirty-six years to King Solomon's death (the temple was dedicated in the fourth year of King Solomon's reign, and he reigned for forty years; 1 Kings 11:42), we have 2,967 years, which takes us to the time when King Solomon's kingdom was divided (2,451 + 480 + 36 = 2,967 years).

After King Solomon died, his kingdom was divided into the Northern Kingdom of Israel and the Southern Kingdom of Judah. The Northern Kingdom was made up of ten of the tribes from the sons of Jacob (Israel). The Southern Kingdom of Judah consisted of the tribe of Judah and Benjamin. The king ruling the Northern Kingdom of Israel was Jeroboam, with Rehoboam ruling the Southern Kingdom of Judah.

Jeroboam did not want his people worshipping at the temple in Jerusalem for fear that they would follow King Rehoboam, so he made golden idols and required the ten tribes to worship them. The Northern Kingdom, Israel, had nineteen kings before being taken into captivity by Assyria, and all the kings of the Northern Kingdom were evil kings who would not serve Jehovah.

Judah had twenty kings with eight good kings, meaning the good kings attempted to rid Judah of all the false gods that Solomon's wives brought into the kingdom. They tried to turn Judah's people back to serving the one and only true God, Jehovah.

If you study the books of 1 and 2 Kings and 1 and 2 Chronicles, you will find the years each king served. Add them up and you will get 374 years from when the kingdom split into the kingdoms of Israel and Judah until the year 606 BC when the kingdom of Judah was taken into captivity in Babylon. The Northern Kingdom went into captivity by Assyria approximately 133 years earlier.

Add 374 years to the 2,967 years we have already calculated to the dividing of Solomon's kingdom, and we have 3,341 years.

God required Judah to remain in captivity in Babylon for seventy years. Why seventy years? God, on the seventh day of creation, established the seventh day as a Sabbath day of rest. He also set the requirements for the sabbath year in Exodus 23:10–12 where he required the Jews to plant their crops for six years, but on the seventh year, they were required to let the ground rest, as this was called the Lord's sabbath. If you look at Genesis 2:1–3, you will see after God finished creating man on the sixth day, he rested on the seventh day not because he was tired but because he was establishing a pattern for humans to follow in their everyday life. We are to work six days each week and rest on the seventh day, and that's when we should set the day apart to worship God. Israel was required to plant their crops for six years, but on the seventh year, God required them to let the land remain unplanted. You see, there is a sabbath for the land as well as for humanity, and God requires His sabbaths to be kept. So how does all this figure into the age of the earth?

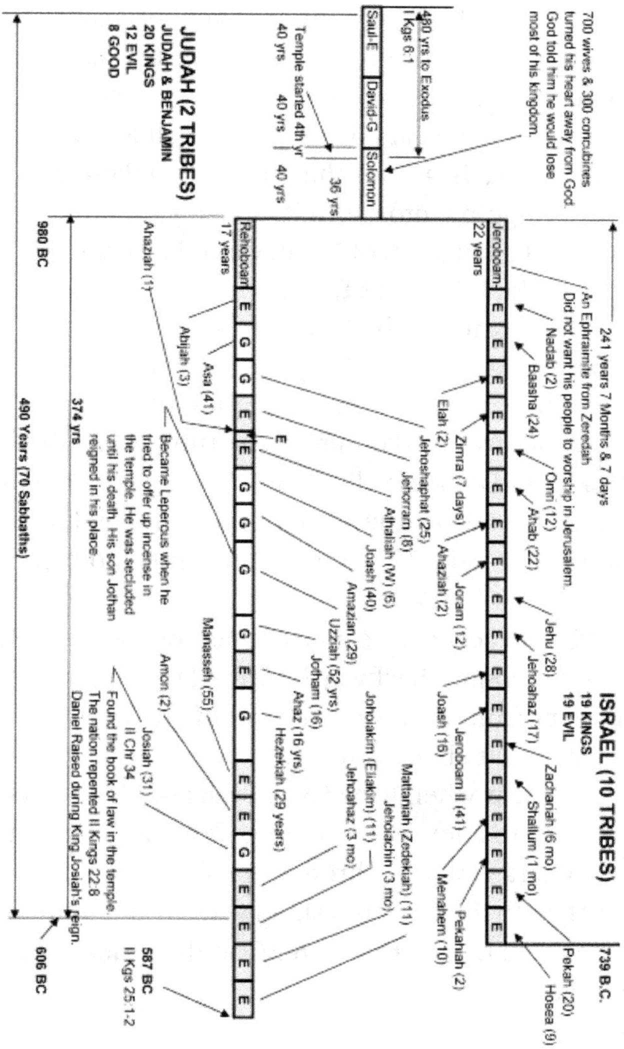

Fig. 10. Judah's kings.

From the fourth year of King Saul, Israel stopped observing the seventh year of sabbath, and this continued thirty-six years under King Saul, forty years under King David, and forty years under King Solomon, plus 374 years with the eighteen kings of Judah, for a total of four hundred ninety years. Remember, God required the sabbath to be observed. It was not an option. God will get His sabbaths owed Him. How many were missed? Four hundred ninety years divided by seven is seventy sabbaths missed; therefore, Israel let the land go unplanted for seventy years. How? By going into captivity in Babylon for seventy years.

In 606 BC, the kingdom of Judah was taken captive in Babylon, and their land laid dormant for seventy years—the exact length of time of the missing sabbaths (2 Chronicles 36:21). God knows how to do the math, and He keeps accurate books.

Let's continue with our determination of the earth's age. We had 2,967 years from Adam up to the time when the kingdoms of Israel and Judah were divided after King Solomon's death. We added 374 years for the reign of the eighteen kings of Judah, which takes us to 606 BC when Judah went into captivity. That totals 3,341 years (2,967 + 374).

If we subtract seventy years from 606 BC, we get 536 BC (remember, time counts backward until AD), which also takes us to 3,411 years from Adam to the end of the captivity of Judah. What is significant about 536 BC?

That is the year when King Cyrus, king of Medo-Persia, issued his first decree to allow the Jews to go back to Judah and rebuild the temple (Ezra 1:1–4; 2 Chronicles 36:23).

We must go to the book of Daniel 9:25 where we find a prophecy that helps us to get from 536 BC to the crucifixion of Christ Jesus in AD 31.

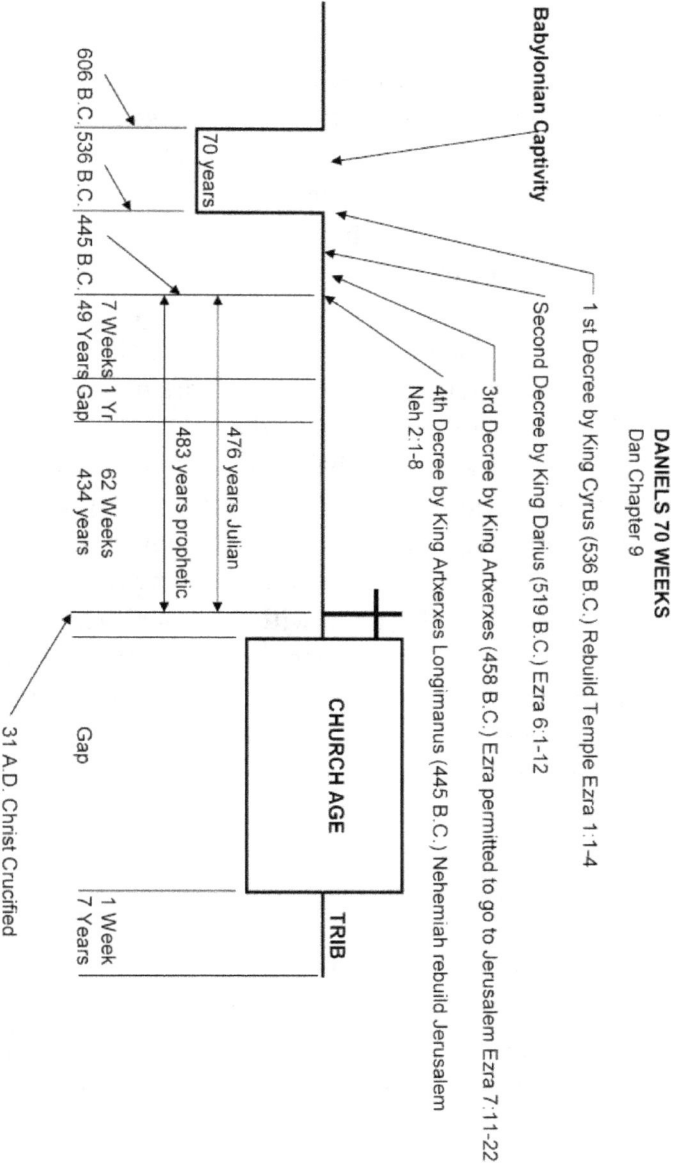

DANIELS 70 WEEKS
Dan Chapter 9

Babylonian Captivity

606 B.C.
536 B.C.
445 B.C.

70 years

7 Weeks 1 Yr
49 Years Gap

62 Weeks
434 years

483 years prophetic

476 years Julian

1 st Decree by King Cyrus (536 B.C.) Rebuild Temple Ezra 1:1-4

Second Decree by King Darius (519 B.C.) Ezra 6:1-12

3rd Decree by King Artxerxes (458 B.C.) Ezra permitted to go to Jerusalem Ezra 7:11-22

4th Decree by King Artxerxes Longimanus (445 B.C.) Nehemiah rebuild Jerusalem
Neh 2:1-8

CHURCH AGE

TRIB

Gap

1 Week
7 Years

31 A.D. Christ Crucified

Fig. 11. Daniel's seventy weeks

In order to calculate the years accurately, we must understand how the calendar works and how God tracks prophetic time. Presently, we use what is called the Gregorian calendar, which was established by a bull issued by Pope Gregory XIII in 1582. The United States adopted the Gregorian calendar in 1652 and at that time had to drop eleven days to line up properly with the calendar. The number of days in one year are 365.25. They make up the 0.25 day every fourth year, which is called a leap year, by adding one day to the month of February.

God, however, measures a year as three hundred sixty days, which we call a prophetic year. Prophecies are measured in three hundred sixty days per year, not 365 days.

I personally have a theory that when God created the earth, He established the orbit as a perfect circle with three hundred sixty degrees, meaning each day the earth moved one degree in the orbit. That would equal three hundred sixty days each year. The earth was spinning like a top without wobbling. It was spinning and orbiting the sun in perfect timing. When Adam and Eve sinned in the garden, the curse came into effect, causing the earth to start wobbling and go into an elliptical orbit we have today. That ended the paradise God created for Adam and Eve to live in.

> We can observe the prophetic year in Genesis 7:11–12 (NKJV), which states, "In the six hundredth year of Noah's life, in the second month, the seventeenth day of the month, on that day all the fountains of the deep were broken up, and the windows of heaven were opened, and the rain was on the earth forty days and forty nights."

On the very same day, Noah and his family entered the ark. All flesh on the earth was destroyed except for Noah and his family (eight in total).

In Genesis 8:3–4 (NKJV) it states,

> "[T]he waters receded continually from the earth. At the end of 150 days the waters decreased. Then the ark rested in the seventh month, the seventeenth day of the month, on the mountains of Ararat."

We can calculate from the second month until the seventh month (five months) equals one hundred fifty days. If we divide one hundred fifty days by five months, we get thirty days in each month, or three hundred sixty days per year. The only way the earth could circle the sun in three hundred sixty days per year would be by having an orbit that is a perfect circle, not an elliptical orbit the earth presently orbits the sun in.

We can verify this also by looking at Revelation 11:2–3 (NKJV) where it states,

> "[B]ut leave out the court which is outside the temple, and do not measure it, for it has been given to the Gentiles. And they will tread the holy city underfoot for forty-two months. And I will give power to my two witnesses, and they will prophesy one thousand two hundred and sixty days (1260 days), clothed in sackcloth."

Forty-two months is 3.5 years. Divide 1,260 days by thirty days per month, and you get 3.5 years; therefore, God counts prophetic time in months containing thirty days.

We must go to Daniel 9:25–26 (NKJV) where he prophesies,

> "Know therefore and understand, that from the going forth of the commandment to restore and build Jerusalem unto the Messiah the Prince shall

be seven weeks, and threescore and two weeks: the street shall be built again, and the wall, even in troublous times. And after threescore and two weeks: shall Messiah shall be cut off, but not for Himself."

Daniel was prophesying that from the decree issued by King Artaxerxes Longimanus letting the Jews go back to Israel to re-build Jerusalem and the walls, issued in 445 BC, to the cutting off of the Messiah or the crucifying of Jesus Christ on Calvary should be a total of sixty-nine weeks (7 + 62 = 69 weeks). In this prophesy, a week is equal to seven years, with a year containing three hundred sixty days each. Since Daniel prophesied there would be seventy weeks total, but after sixty-nine weeks were accomplished God's time clock stopped with one week or seven years remaining after the Messiah was cut off. The time period from the crucifixion of Jesus until present is called the church age or the age of grace and when it is complete, God will once again start the time clock of prophecy to fulfill the last seven years. Those seven years being the time of the tribulation or the time of Jacobs trouble. This will occur after the rapture of the church and start the clock ticking on the seven years of tribulation before the millennium kingdom begins with Christ Jesus as king.

But we are considering the sixty-nine weeks of Daniel's prophecy in our present calculations. Sixty-nine weeks represent 483 years, but using the Gregorian calendar, we only have 476 years from 445 BC to AD 31. How do we resolve this difference? We convert years to days. Four hundred eighty-three prophetic years multiplied by three hundred sixty days per year gives us 173,880 days divided by 365.25 days in a Gregorian calendar year equals 476 years and twenty-one days. Remember, Daniel's prophecy was divided into seven weeks plus sixty-two weeks. We do not know what the gap between the first seven weeks and the sixty-two weeks represents, but it could be the small amount of time (twenty-one days). So, let's bring our timeline up to date.

Let's go back to our last benchmark where we took 606 BC and subtracted seventy years of captivity for the kingdom of Judah, giving us the year 536 BC. This is when King Cyrus issued the decree letting the Jews go back and rebuild the temple. There was a total of four decrees issued by the kings of Persia.

1. King Cyrus's decree to rebuild the temple in 536 BC (Ezra 1:1–4).
2. King Darius's decree as shown in Ezra 6:1–12 occurring in 519 BC (reiterates King Cyrus's decree in Ezra 1:1–4).
3. King Artaxerxes's decree where Ezra was allowed to go to Jerusalem in 458 BC (Ezra 7:11–22).
4. King Artaxerxes Longimanus's decree allowing Nehemiah to go rebuild Jerusalem in 445 BC (Nehemiah 2:1–8).

Taking the 445 BC decree and subtracting 445 BC from 536 BC, we get ninety-one more years, which added to 3,411 years from Adam to the end of captivity of Judah. We have 3,502 years from Adam to the decree in 445 BC coinciding with the prophecy of Daniel 9:25. Now, if we add 3,502 years and 476 years, taking us to AD 31 when Jesus was crucified, we have 3,978 years. This book is being written in 2019, so we subtract thirty-one years from 2019, and we have 1,988 years from the crucifixion to 2019. Add that number of years to 3,978 years, and the age of the earth is 5,966 years.

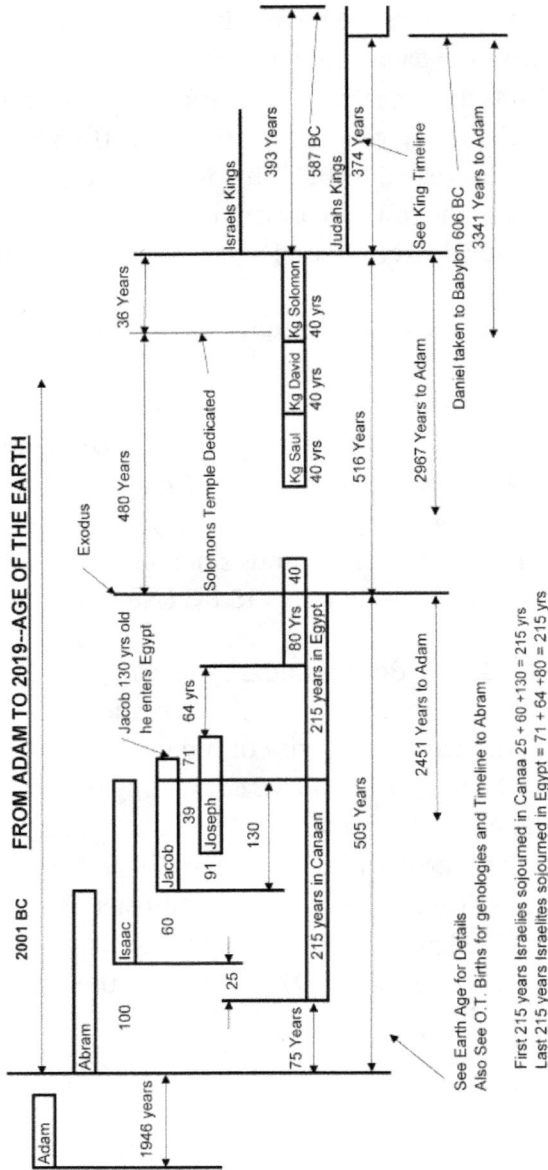

Fig. 12. From Adam to the captivity of Judah.

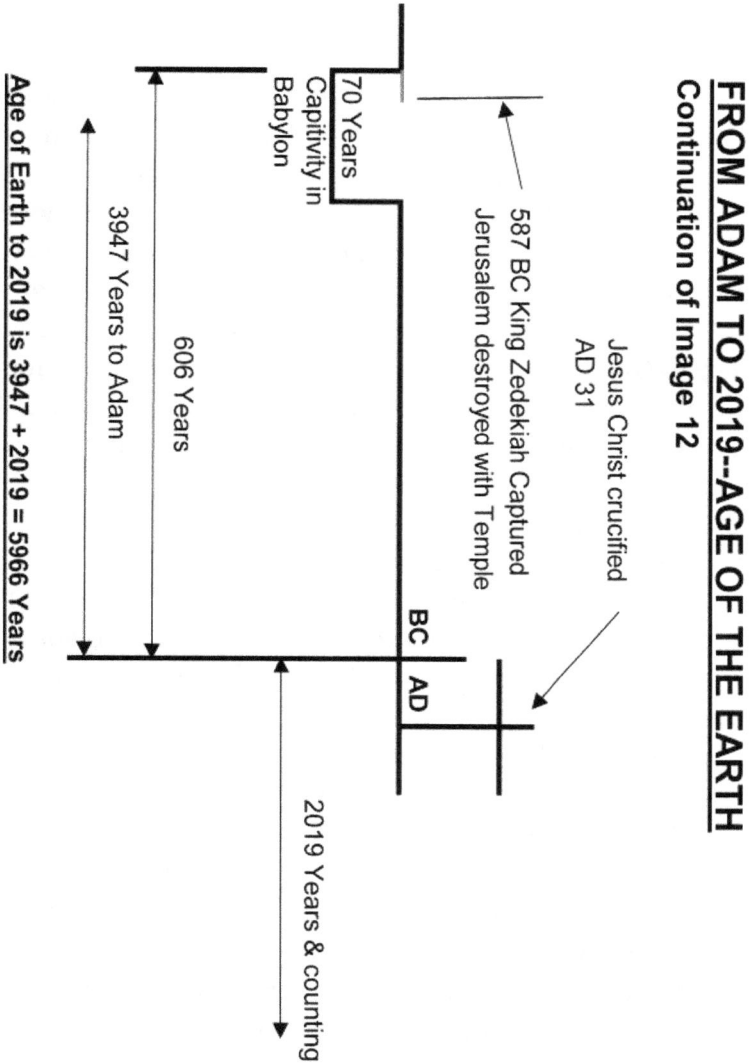

FROM ADAM TO 2019--AGE OF THE EARTH

Continuation of Image 12

Jesus Christ crucified
AD 31

587 BC King Zedekiah Captured
Jerusalem destroyed with Temple

70 Years
Capitivity in
Babylon

3947 Years to Adam

606 Years

Age of Earth to 2019 is 3947 + 2019 = 5966 Years

BC

AD

2019 Years & counting

Fig. 13. From Judah's captivity.

So, the next time you turn on the Discovery Channel and a so-called scientist picks up a rock and says that it's seven billion years old, you know that person does not know the truth. As

I have said before, true science and true scientists require empirical evidence for the theories they are proclaiming as true. Three or four hundred years ago, scientists believed the Bible and believed in God as the creator, and their theories were proven or unproven by empirical evidence. Today, most scientists do not believe in God as the creator, nor do they accept the Holy Bible as the Word of God; therefore, we have godless theories proclaimed as true without evidence or proof, and we are supposed to just accept what they say. Well, I for one want to see the evidence. Global warming (climate change) is another unproven theory that has become political; and mark my word, it will cost us billions and billions in tax dollars and penalties to fund their projects, and what will be the result? Rich politicians and businesses lining their pockets with your money and my money. There are scientists out there trying to tell the truth, and you know what happens, their data and information is taken off the Internet. They, the politicians, don't want the truth to come out because it will show it is all a scheme to make a few very rich while the multitude pays the bill. If carbon dioxide is so bad for the atmosphere, why do the people who promote removing carbon dioxide from the atmosphere live in huge energy-eating and carbon-dioxide-producing homes. Why do they fly in private jets expelling deadly chemicals and carbon dioxide in the atmosphere thousands of times the carbon dioxide you and I would expel in a year? They don't even want the cows to let off gas, which is a food source. For the first 1,654 years after creation, humans did not eat meat, nor did the animals. That would mean the animal population on the earth must have been many times what it is today, and yet God was not worried about all these animals letting off gas and producing an overabundance of carbon dioxide. Climate change is a man made narrative to make billions of dollars for a few. Sadly, multitudes are also speaking out that climate change is true because it has been drilled into their brains from kindergarten through college. They won't discuss or listen to an argument that counters climate change. Do you think the leaders of this movement avoid eating steak? No! They just want everybody else to stop eating steak—the same way with electricity for their homes and gas for their jets.

Sadly, our children are being taught these godless theories, so is it any wonder our culture and society are moving away from anything referring to a loving God and Savior Jesus Christ. Ninety-nine people out of a hundred on the street do not have a clue what God says in His Word, yet they believe every word spoken over the Discovery Channel or by their college professor.

Our society is becoming confrontational and angry. You have to be careful how you approach people today or they will lash out at you and may even become violent. God help us.

Regardless, I believe God placed such detail of the genealogies in His word to provide evidence the earth is 5966 years old and counting.

CHAPTER 9

The Fall of Mankind

P eople ask many times why we have to suffer under a curse that began with Adam and Eve. They say they are not guilty of the sin of Adam and Eve, so why should they be punished for a sin they did not commit? It causes them to curse God and believe that He is unjust in His dealings with mankind. Our study in this chapter will show that we are all guilty of the original sin of Adam and therefore are in line for God's judgment unless we confess (admit) our sins and sin nature and accept Jesus Christ as our Lord and Savior by faith.

First, we must recognize how Satan works to trap and deceive all of us. No one is exempt. What tools does Satan use to get us to falter and fail?

We are all made with five senses or gates that Satan tries to infiltrate in some manner. We have eyes for seeing, ears for hearing, a nose for smelling, a mouth for tasting and communicating, and the sense of touch for feeling. First John 2:15–16 tells us, "Love not the world, neither the things that are in the world. If any man love the world, the love of the Father is not in him. For all that is in the world, the lust of the flesh, the lust of the eyes, and the pride of life, is not of the Father, but is of the world."

In Genesis 3:1–6, we find Satan appearing to Eve as a serpent. Many theologians place Adam right beside Eve when she was tempted, but I disagree. Adam was not present at this time because if he was, Satan would have spoken to Adam and not Eve. Why? Because Adam was the federal head of the human race, not Eve. She was his helpmeet. Had Satan tried to talk to Eve rather than Adam, he would have been ignoring the federal head of the human race as created by God. Adam was created first, and Eve was made from a rib God took from Adam's side. This occurred after Adam named all the animals, then he saw the animals with their mates. He felt lonely. God saw Adam's loneliness and decided to give him a helpmeet (Genesis 2:18). Eve was in submission to Adam just like God originally set up marriage between a man and a woman. Adam was the head of the family and the federal head of the human race; therefore, if he was present at the temptation, he would have stepped in and stopped it as he had firsthand instruction from God to not partake of the fruit from the tree of knowledge of good and evil.

So, we have Eve alone with the serpent in the garden of Eden. Now, God had instructed Adam that he and Eve could eat from all the trees in the garden except the tree in the midst of the garden called the tree of the knowledge of good and evil (Genesis 2:16–17). I would like to note here that there was another tree in the garden that is very important, the tree of life (Genesis 2:9). They could partake of that tree along with all the others except for the tree of knowledge of good and evil. The tree of life perpetuated their lives as long as they ate from it.

In Genesis 3:1–5, we have the discourse between Satan and Eve, which is in effect an ear gate attack by Satan. Satan lied to Eve, "Hath God said, 'Ye shall not eat of every tree of the garden?'" Eve tried to answer him by stating, "We may eat of the fruit of the trees of the garden." She went on to say, "[B]ut of the fruit of the tree which is in the midst of the garden, God hath said, 'Ye shall not eat of it, neither shall ye touch it, lest you die.'" The serpent said, "Ye shall not surely die." In other words, Satan was calling God a liar. For he went on in verse 5 to say, "For God doth know that in the day ye eat thereof, then your eyes shall be opened, and ye shall be as gods, knowing good and evil."

Now, notice what happens in verse 6 Satan had Eve look upon the fruit of the tree to see how good and appealing it was to her eyes. This is an eye gate attack. That's one reason Las Vegas has all the neon lights on the strip. It is so appealing to the eye. It just draws you into the bars and casinos where they will remove your money from you and leave you broke, drunk, and miserable. People will continue to go back for the glamour and excitement because their eyes tell them it is so much fun. Afterwards comes the hangover and the realization they are broke. When Eve saw that the fruit was good for food and would make her wise, she ate the fruit. Satan had deceived Eve. This is evident as stated in 1 Timothy 2:14,

> "And Adam was not deceived, but the woman be-
> ing deceived was in the transgression."

After Eve ate the fruit, Adam came on the scene and imme-diately saw what Eve had done, and it must have shocked him to the core. He was aware what God had said. This was a death sentence for Eve. To understand Adam's feelings at this moment and to have understanding of his actions thereafter, we need to look at Exodus 21:2–6 concerning the law pertaining to bondser-vants. Verse 2 says,

> "If thou buy an Hebrew servant, six years he shall
> serve: and in the seventh year he shall go out free
> and for nothing."

These servants must be men who owe a debt and are sold or volunteer to go into servanthood to settle the debt through work. Verse 3 says,

"If he came in by himself, he shall go out by himself: if he were married, then his wife shall go out with him."

Verse 4, and here is Adam's dilemma,

"If his master have given him a wife, and she have born him sons or daughters; the wife and her children shall be her master's, and he shall go out by himself."

Can you imagine a man wanting his freedom so bad he could taste it and he is almost to the seventh year when he realizes his wife given to him by his master and his children cannot go with him? It would rip his heart out to walk away from them. That's the feeling Adam experienced when he wanted so badly to follow God's command and have fellowship with him, but his love for Eve was so great that he was willing to take the death sentence along with her rather than obey God. So, he ate the fruit. Now the death here could be on two fronts. One is physical, the death that immediately started working in their bodies under the curse, and the second death was a spiritual death when they were separated from God's fellowship. The relationship had been broken. The curse was in effect as it is today. Adam was not deceived into eating the fruit, but his action was willful sin against God's strict command to abstain from eating the fruit from just that one tree. In other words, Adam knew what he was doing and chose to go against God's instructions. Today, we see people go against the instruction laid down in the Bible as to how we should live our lives. God knows what is best for us, and he wants us to be successful and obedient, but it is our choice. Many people today are taking the wrong road and making bad choices. Here's just one example of how disobedient people are today. A young man who can't seem to keep a job must depend on a friend to give him a place to live. While there, he meets a young lady, they have sex, and she becomes pregnant. Now they want to get married. This seems to be the trend these days. I call it getting the cart before the horse. They are not using wisdom in their decisions, just doing what their flesh wants. Here is a man starting a family and he can't even provide a home for himself. What is the child going to experience when it is born? Back to Adam and Eve, God did not require much from Adam and Eve, and He does not require much from us, just obedience. Now we see God take action. In Genesis 3:15, God deals with the serpent Satan where He tells the serpent he will be cursed more than all the other animals and will crawl on his belly and eat the dust of the earth. Here is the first prophetic statement in the Bible where God tells Satan that he (Satan) will bruise the heel of the women's Seed, referring to the crucifixion of Jesus Christ on the cross, but that the women's Seed will crush the head of the serpent Satan, meaning at the appointed time, God the Son, Jesus Christ, will have one of His angels cast Satan in the lake of fire for eternity where the anti-Christ and the false prophet will be (Revelation 20:10). Next, we see why God drove Adam and Eve from the garden after they sinned. In Genesis 3:22–23 it states,

> "And the Lord God said, 'Behold, the man is become as one of us, to know good and evil: and now, lest he put forth his hand, and take also of the tree of life, and eat, and live forever': Therefore the Lord God sent him forth from the garden of Eden, to till the ground from whence he was taken."

God drove Adam and Eve out of the garden to prevent them from eating fruit from the tree of life lest they live forever in their sinful state. Had they done that, the need for Christ Jesus to be sacrificed for their sins could not be accomplished, for they would have lived forever. One thing the sin of Adam brought into the world was death. Scientists want us to believe that dinosaurs and humans lived on the earth millions of years ago and that the dinosaurs died out sixty-million years ago. If that were true, then death would have existed before Adam and Eve sinned. The Bible clearly teaches that death was part of the curse brought into existence by their sin and disobedience. Romans 5:12 states,

> "Wherefore, as by one-man sin entered into the world, and death by sin; and so death passed upon all men, for that all have sinned."

So, God set cherubim to watch over the garden and keep them out. What an awful change in relationship between God and humans. A relationship of walking in the garden in the evening talking to God directly, then to be driven out of the garden paradise and having to till the ground by the sweat of his brow. Women would bring forth children with much pain. Yes! That's part of the curse. So, how does all this make us guilty of Adam's sin? To determine how we are guilty of the original sin, we must go to Genesis 14 where we find four kings (Amrapel, Aroich, Chedorlaomer, and Tidal) coming against five kings (Bera, Birsha, Shinab, Shemeber, and Zoar). Bera was king of Sodom, and Birsha was king of Gomorrah. Now the four attacking kings were victorious over the five kings, and they were in servitude to King Chedorlaomer for twelve years. On the thirteenth year, they rebelled, and the fight took place in the Valley of the Salt Sea (the Dead Sea). A messenger fled and notified Abraham that his nephew Lot had been taken captive. Abraham had 318 servants who saddled up and went to battle defeating King Chadorlaomer and freeing Lot, Abraham's nephew, along with all his people and their possessions. On the return trip, King Melchizedek, king of Salem, which we know as Jerusalem, came out to meet Abraham and bless him. Abraham paid a tithe to King Melchizedek from all he had, and King Melchizedek blessed Abraham. Then the king from Sodom came out to meet Abraham and asked him to return all his people but to keep all the spoil he had taken. Abraham returned all the people and all the possessions belonging to the king, as he would not take anything belonging to that king. We have seen that Abraham paid a tithe to King Melchizedek, so what significance does this have concerning the original sin of Adam being attributed to us? For the answer, we must turn to Hebrews 7:9–10 where it states,

> "Even Levi, who receives tithes because he was a priest, paid tithes through Abraham, so to speak, for he was still in the loins of his father when Melchizedek met him."

So, something your father or even grandfather did can be attributed to you. I know this sounds weird, but just as God attributed the tithe of Abraham to the account of Levi (the tribe where the priests come from), so God places the sin of Adam into our accounts because we all were in the loins of our father Adam (the first man) when he committed the act of rebelling against God and choosing to go the way of Eve by eating the forbidden fruit. This is how you and I are guilty of the original sin along with Adam and Eve. But God does not leave us in this state of a sin burden even though we all have a sin nature. Because of His mercy, love, and grace, He provides a way to get back into fellowship with Him. Genesis 3:15 shows us that at the very moment He confronts Adam and Eve and the serpent (Satan), He expresses a prophetic statement announcing the coming Savior Jesus Christ, His Son. Genesis 3:15 states,

> "And I will put enmity between you and the women, and between your seed and her Seed; He shall bruise your head and you shall bruise His heal."

Here we have the first prophetic statement in the Bible concerning the coming Messiah. In just twenty-eight words, God shows there will be deep-seated hostility between the woman and Satan. Notice when the Scripture refers to Satan's seed it has a small "s," but when it mentions the women's seed, it has a capital "S" indicating the women's seed will be Jesus Christ our Lord and Savior. That's why all references in this book of God the father, God the Son (Jesus) and God the Holy Spirit are capitalized (He, Him, His, etc.) The verse in Genesis 3:15 also shows the war that will exist between Satan and the Lord Jesus Christ. It shows Satan bruising the Lord's heel (crucifixion), while the Lord will bruise Satan's head (final defeat). You know that victory goes to the one who wounds his foe in the head versus the one who wounds his foe in the heel. Satan will one day be cast into the lake of fire as a final defeat. We can rejoice and find comfort in knowing that although we are all guilty of original sin, God in His goodness and mercy immediately proclaimed a Savior would come from the Seed of women. This occurred through the birth of Jesus Christ the Son of God through the virgin Mary. Jesus, the Son of God, went to the cross and died in my place and your place as a perfect sacrifice to redeem us from our sin debt, as only He could as the perfect sacrifice. If it ended in His death it would have been sad, but death could not hold Him, and after three days in the tomb, He came out and showed Himself to over five hundred witnesses and the apostles before ascending into the heavens to sit at the right hand of the Father. He sits there now as our high priest and intercessor interceding for you and me. Praise the Lord.

CHAPTER 10

The Cross and the Blood

As I stated in the previous chapter, Genesis 3:15 is a prophetic verse stating God would provide a Seed (the Savior) from a woman who would bruise the head, or defeat, our foe Satan. We need to understand that mankind's bloodline has been polluted, starting with Adam, by the sin nature, and it is passed down through the father(s) to all offspring. Romans 5:18–19 states,

> "Therefore as by the offence of one judgment came upon all men to condemnation; even so by the righteousness of one the free gift came upon all men unto justification of life. For as by one man's disobedience many were made sinners, so by the obedience of one shall many be made righteous."

We all are guilty of the original sin along with Adam, and we all need a savior to get saved. God requires a perfect sacrifice to settle the sin debt. Jewish law shows us an example of that where they are required to sacrifice a lamb without blemish on the altar. To do this, they would select the best of all their flock(s) and separate them for three days to see if anything showed up to make them unworthy of sacrifice. If no blemishes appeared, they would take the lamb to slaughter. All of this was a forerunner of God providing the perfect sacrifice for humanity's sin nature. If humans are not worthy, then God must provide His own sacrifice to deal with the sin problem. God the Holy Spirit impregnated a young virgin named Mary who would give birth to baby Jesus in Bethlehem. I must explain how the blood that circulated in Jesus's veins was pure, versus the blood that circulates in your veins and my veins. I have already explained how we are guilty of original sin by being in the loins of Adam when he committed the original sin. Our bloodline is polluted with sin and unworthy of satisfying the sin debt. Now, let's consider how God provided a pure bloodline through Jesus. When pregnant, a woman has a placenta attached to the wall of her uterus, which provides nourishment to the fetus by means of osmosis. In other words, the life-giving food in the mother's blood stream transfers through a membrane in the placenta to the child's umbilical cord and into the child's stomach, then into its bloodstream just like we process food in our bodies today. The woman's blood never touches the child's blood; therefore, it is possible to have a pure bloodline if the father's blood is pure. Mary's blood was not pure because of the curse. God the Holy Spirit impregnated Mary; therefore, Jesus was born with a pure bloodline free of the original sin nature. It's all about the blood. I should note here that our blood carries life. Blood is not life but carries life. This is evident when someone dies, the body is still warm after expiration and will remain so for a while, yet the person is dead because the life has departed from the blood. The life of humanity is carried in his blood stream. Life itself is spiritual but needs a carrier, and that is the blood. The physical contact between the divine and the human rests in the blood stream. You can put blood in a bottle, even freeze it, and when it is warmed and injected into a person's bloodstream, it sustains that person's life. You can put an African American's blood in a White person or vice versa, and it doesn't matter as long as the blood is the same type. So, how did Jesus have a sinless nature? Dr. William Standish Reed of the Christian Medical Foundation of Tampa, Florida, writes, "The female ovum itself has no blood, neither does the male Spermatozoon; but it is when these two come together in the fallopian tube that's when conception takes place, and a new life begins." That's why abortion is the killing of a living human being and should be called murder. At this writing, there are at least two states approving murdering a child after it leaves the mother's body. That is murder, and the mother and the doctor should be prosecuted.

Let me digress for a minute on a very important issue. Women's choice. I have become aware through the news media that our government is sending up to and maybe more than five-hundred million dollars to support Planned Parenthood. I have thought about this, and here's how I would equate what our government is doing. During World War II, Hitler so hated the Jewish people that he established factories to eliminate them from the face of the earth. Six million Jews were killed by those factories, and it was paid for by government funds. Every German citizen helped pay for the killing of the Jews through their tax dollars. Tell me, what is the difference between the German government funding death camps and the US government funding Planned Parenthood to set up killing factories? Further, Hitler had his people remove anything of value from the Jews before killing them (i.e., skin, hair, gold teeth, clothes, shoes). This occurred after he used them for slave labor until they were no longer useful. Planned Parenthood is removing hearts, lungs, and any organ of value so they can sell them to research centers in the name of medical progress. Do you see the similarity? We are just as guilty as the German government and the German people letting their government do what they did. As far as women's choice is concerned, we as a nation have gone too far in the name of "women's choice." A woman's choice ends at the sex act. She has the choice to say no or to use contraceptives, but she should never have been given the right to choose to kill her unborn child. Young women can choose to give up their child for adoption and avoid being guilty of murder, but we as a nation have made it convenient to kill the baby.

Now back to the blood. Leviticus 17:11 states,

> "For the life of the flesh is in the blood, and I have given it to you upon the altar to make atonement for your souls; for it is the blood that makes atonement for the soul."

The blood cells in this new creation are from both the father and mother, and the blood type is determined at the moment of conception and is therefore protected by the placenta from any flow of blood from the mother into the fetus. Now, we find that Mary was impregnated by the Holy Spirit, and since her blood did not circulate through the veins of Jesus, He was born sinless because God the Father was sinless. Four things we know occurred when the Holy Spirit impregnated the virgin Mary:

1. Her blood did not flow into the veins of Jesus.
2. Jesus did not have an earthly father to pass the curse on to Him.
3. Therefore, Jesus was born sinless.
4. He alone was worthy to atone for the sins of mankind.

Jesus took all the sins of mankind and hung them on the cross and thereby provides redemption from the curse of sin for everyone who will accept Jesus as their Lord and Savior. His pure, sinless blood ran down that old wooden cross, and it is at the cross where we can have our sins blotted out by the blood of Jesus. In Matthew 26:28 Jesus said,

"For this is My blood of the new covenant, which is shed for many for the remission of sins."

In Luke 22:20 NKJV, likewise He also took the cup after supper, saying,

"This is the new covenant in My blood, which is shed for you."

John 6:54 says,

"Whoever eats My flesh and drinks My blood has eternal life, and I will raise him up at the last day."

Hebrews 9:22 says,

"And almost all things are by the law purged with blood, and without shedding of blood there is no remission."

The blood is the atonement for sin, so the church cannot leave the blood out of its message. If they do, they might as well close their doors. Today there is a movement in the churches to remove the cross and not mention the blood. Why? They say it is because it is offensive to the lost sinner. Now think about sinners. What do they watch on TV to entertain themselves? Blood and guts. They can't get the shows gory enough for the audience. The more blood and guts and extreme action, the larger the audience. And the bigger the profits the moviemakers get.

I love the old cowboy movies and watch them when I can. But modern-day western movies are so filled with blood and guts they are hard to watch. Some of them I can't watch. In the old westerns, a man got shot and there was no blood. Many times, when they got shot in the shoulder, they just got on their horse and started fighting and shooting again. They sort of forgot the pain, but it was a good story line and good entertainment.

Today, even the video games your children play are filled with blood and guts. So, don't tell me the church should do away with the blood and the cross. It just doesn't compute. Don't tell me the blood that Jesus shed on the cross may offend people or turn their stomach when our society today entertains themselves on blood and guts.

The precious blood of Jesus is holy and pure, and God the Father sent Jesus for the purpose of providing an atonement for your sins and my sins. We should praise and worship God daily for the blood of Jesus. Satan has worked his way into the hearts of many preachers to the point that they don't want to preach about the death, burial, and resurrection of Jesus Christ our Lord and Savior, which is the essence of the gospel of grace according to 1 Corinthians 15:1–4:

> "Moreover, brethren, I declare unto you the gospel which I preached unto you, which also ye have received, and wherein, ye stand; By which also ye are saved, if ye keep in memory what I preached unto you, unless ye have believed in vain. For I delivered unto you first of all that which I also received, how that Christ died for our sins according to the scriptures; And that He was buried, and that He rose again the third day according to the scriptures."

They would rather preach about feel-good things like:

1. Just think about how good you are.
2. God wants you to be rich.
3. Do what feels good today.
4. There are many ways to heaven.

5. Jesus is not the only way.
6. Subjective things, like your destiny or legacy.

They would rather promote the church by serving hot dogs and hamburgers and pony rides than promote the one who can save their souls by His sacrifice on the cross. Many churches are even promoting that there are several ways to get to Heaven other than by accepting Jesus as their Lord and Savior. This is straight out of the Eastern religions. Acts 4:12 tells us there is no other name under heaven whereby humans can be saved except the name of Jesus. Jesus himself said in John 14:6,

> "I am the way, the truth, and the life. No one comes to the Father except through Me."

The missionaries in Africa used to say, "The natives would not listen to the gospel preached until they were fed." The problem is that the church feeds the public but does not preach the salvation message. The people leave with full stomachs and have not heard the gospel. Some of our quartets are canceling engagements because the churches they are scheduled to sing at won't let them give their testimony or mention the name of Jesus or the blood. Quartets are having churches cancel them because they are singing about the cross and the blood. What a shameful condition the church is in today. You might as well write "Ickabod" over their door(s). Let us always preach the death, burial, and the resurrection of Jesus as our Lord and Savior. First Corinthians 15:1–4 presents the gospel to us when it states,

> "Moreover, brethren, I declare unto you the gospel which I preached unto you, which also ye have received, and wherein ye stand; by which also ye are saved, if ye keep in memory what I preached unto you, unless ye have believed in vain. For I

delivered unto you first of all that which I also received, how that Christ died for our sins according to the scriptures; and that He was buried, and
that He rose again the third day according to the
scriptures."

I repeated this scripture because this is the gospel we need to
preach. The blood cannot be measured in dollars and cents. The
blood of Jesus is priceless. When the temple was dedicated, the
number of animals could not be numbered. A stream of blood
ran in the Kidron Valley for days. In 1 Kings 8:5, a peace offering
was made for the nation of Israel, and twenty-two thousand oxen
and one hundred twenty thousand sheep were sacrificed. Why
not just one little lamb? God is trying to impress on all of us the
value of the blood. No amount of blood from animals in the Old
Testament could atone for our sin. All of the animal sacrifices in
the Old Testament pointed to a coming Messiah (Jesus Christ)
who would be the perfect sacrifice and end the need for further
sacrifices. Hebrews 9:22 tells us that

"without the shedding of blood there is no remission of sins."

When Jesus shed His blood, it opened a fountain of blood that
will never run dry. His blood does not cover our sins; it blots
them out. Our sins are tossed into the sea of forgetfulness never
to be brought up against us again. You might say that Jesus posts
a "no fishing" sign next to that sea. So, remember this, if you have
sinned, there is a fount of blood that never runs dry; and if you
allow Jesus to wash you in His blood, your sins, no matter how
bad or how many, will be forgiven you. Praise the Lord!

Here are the scriptures the lost person needs to read to understand our condition and the solution for it, which is giving our
life to Jesus Christ.

How to get saved:

1. Salvation for those who Believe (Romans 1:16).
2. God leads us to Repentance (Romans 2:4).
3. All have sinned (Romans 3:23).
4. While we were sinners, Christ died for us (Romans 5:8).
5. The wages of sin is death (Romans 6:23).
6. Confess Jesus with your mouth (Romans 10:9).
7. Whosoever calls on the name of the Lord shall be saved (Romans 10:13).

If you are not saved and want to get saved, pray this prayer with me and sincerely mean what you say.

> Lord Jesus, I am a lost sinner and want you to save my soul. I confess that I have sinned against you and your Word, but I believe you are truly the Son of God, and I repent of my sinful life and ask you to forgive me of all my sins. I accept you as my Lord and Savior today and will serve you the rest of my life. Thank you, Lord, that according to your Word I am now saved, and I can call myself a Christian. Amen.

If you sincerely prayed that prayer and mean it in your heart, the angels in heaven are rejoicing, for a new creature was just born according to 2 Corinthians 5:17–18,

"Therefore if any man, be in Christ, he is a new creature; old things are passed away; behold, all things are become new, and all things are of God, who hath reconciled us to himself by Jesus Christ, and hath given us the ministry of reconciliation."

Congratulations!

CHAPTER 11

Paradise Empty

Years ago, I had a fellow worker who invited me to a new synagogue that was being opened to the public for a short period of time. They were going to have a service where they held a baptism for the dead. If you haven't figured out what church I am referring to by now, it is the Mormon Church. I thanked the man and told him I did not believe in praying for the dead to get them out of paradise and into heaven. I believe paradise in the lower parts of the earth is empty today. Saints in paradise in heaven do not need our prayers. Let me explain. He wanted to have a dialogue with me using the Book of Mormon, but I told him the only basis he and I had to discuss scriptural issues would be the Word of God in the King James Bible (the Mormons say they believe the Bible is the Word of God), and not the Mormon Church's books. In the Old Testament times, there was a paradise located in the lower parts of the earth, just as there was and still is a place called hell located in the lower parts of the earth. Paradise is where the souls of Old Testament saints went when they died. They did not go directly to heaven. They were held in waiting for a very important event. In fact, I would say it was the most important event in the history of the world. That means Abraham, Isaac, Jacob, and all the other Old Testament saints were in paradise in the lower parts of the earth when Jesus died on the cross. What great event were they held there for? The coming of the Messiah, Jesus Christ the Son of God. Jesus was the perfect sacrifice to redeem mankind from their sins. Do we have evidence of this? Yes! I will explain in just a moment, but first I would also like to establish that there is a paradise in heaven as Paul shows us in 2 Corinthians 12:4 where he states,

> "How that he was caught up into paradise, and heard unspeakable words."

Notice, Paul was caught up, not down, meaning in Paul's day, paradise was located in heaven and not in the lower parts of the earth. Also, in Revelation 2:7, we have,

> "He that hath an ear, let him hear what the Spirit saith unto the churches; To him that overcometh will I give to eat of the tree of life, which is located in the midst of the paradise of God."

These two verses show us where paradise is today, and we can look forward to going there. Let's turn our attention to the old empty paradise located in the lower parts of the earth. The paradise in the bowels of the earth was the one Jesus referred to on the cross when he spoke to the repentant sinner stating in Luke 23:43,

> "And Jesus said unto him, Verily I say unto thee, today shalt thou be with me in paradise."

We know that Jesus did not ascend to heaven (the heavenly paradise) when he died on the cross but was buried and went to paradise located in the lower parts of the earth as shown in Ephesians 4:9,

"Now that he ascended, what is it but that he also descended first into the lower parts of the earth?"

Why did Jesus go into the lower paradise? First Peter 4:6 states,

"For this cause was the gospel preached also to them that are dead, that they might be judged according to men in the flesh, but live according to God in the spirit."

That the Old Testament saints might accept Jesus as Messiah. Paradise in the lower parts of the earth was where the Old Testament righteous dead went as shown in Luke 16:22–31:

And it came to pass, that the beggar died, and was carried by the angels into Abraham's bosom: the rich man also died, and was buried; And in hell he lift up his eyes, being in torments, and seeth Abraham afar off, and Lazarus in his bosom. And he cried and said, Father Abraham, have mercy on me, and send Lazarus, that he may dip the tip of his finger in water, and cool my tongue; for I am tormented in this flame. But Abraham said, Son, remember that thou in thy lifetime receivedst thy good things, and likewise Lazarus evil things: but now he is comforted, and thou art tormented. And beside all this, between us and you there is a great gulf fixed: so that they which would pass from hence to you cannot; neither can they pass to us, that would come from thence. Then he said, I pray thee therefore, father, that thou wouldest send him to my father's house: For I have five brethren; that he may testify unto them, lest they also come into this place of torment. Abraham saith unto him, they have Moses and the prophets; let them hear them. And he said, Nay, father Abraham: but if one went unto them from the dead, they will repent. And he said unto him, if they hear not Moses and the prophets, neither will they be persuaded, though one rose from the dead.

We see in these verses a picture of a lost soul in hell looking over a great gulf into paradise where the righteous saints were held waiting for the Messiah to come and preach to them with the result that they all accepted Jesus as their Lord and Savior. Jesus's blood shed on Calvary blotted out their sins once and for all. No one can stand before God justified without the atoning blood of Jesus to blot out their sins, not even the Old Testament righteous saints who were in paradise on the day of Christ's death. The way to heaven is by the blood of Jesus as stated in Acts 4:10–12,

"Be it known unto you all, and to all the people of Israel, that by the name of Jesus Christ of Nazareth, whom ye crucified, whom God raised from the dead, even by him doth this man stand here before you whole. This is the stone which was set at nought of you builders, which is become the head of the corner. Neither is there salvation in any other: for there is none other name under heaven given among men, whereby we must be saved."

The Old Testament saints were held in reserve until the promised Messiah came. Their sins had been covered by the blood of animals (an act performed once a year at the temple in Jerusalem). Hebrews 10:3–4 says,

"But in those sacrifices there is a remembrance again made of sins every year. For it is not possible that the blood of bulls and of goats should take away sins."

Their sins were merely covered by the blood of the animals they sacrificed. They needed the Savior just as you and I do today. They needed the blood of Jesus to blot out their sins the same as you and I do today. Jesus died on the cross, was buried in a borrowed tomb, He then went down into the lower paradise and presented Himself as the promised Messiah. The saints there accepted Jesus as their Lord and Savior, and that put them in position to be taken with him to the upper paradise in heaven. They, however, could not go to paradise in heaven until He ascended to heaven to present His shed blood in the holy of holies in the temple in heaven, then return to earth. Jesus rose from the dead, and He is the first fruits from the grave. It stands to reason that if the Old Testament saints had their sins blotted out and are now in heaven with Jesus, and if New Testament saints are instantly in the presence of Christ, as Paul indicates in Philippians 1:23–24,

"For I am in a strait betwixt two, having a desire to depart, and to be with Christ; which is far better: Nevertheless to abide in the flesh is more needful for you,"

there is no need for the lower paradise. It was emptied upon Christ's resurrection and ascension where it states in Ephesians 4:8,

"Wherefore He saith, When He ascended up on high, He led captivity captive, and gave gifts unto men."

Those Old Testament saints held captive were now being led by Christ to paradise in heaven. Now let's consider how all this took place. The Old Testament saints went to paradise in the lower parts of the earth when they died. It must have been a place of enjoyment and comfort as a reward for their faith in God. As I said before, the Old Testament saints could not precede Jesus in His resurrection and ascension to heaven. They could not go to heaven without receiving Him as the Messiah. They must accept Him as their Savior. Acts 4:12 tells us,

> "There is no other name under Heaven whereby man may be saved, except the name of Jesus."

Jesus was crucified on the cross of Calvary, was buried, and remained in the grave for three days. During that time, He made a trip to paradise in the lower part of the earth to present himself as the Messiah. The saints there accepted Jesus as their Savior, and His blood blotted out their sins. At that time, He was not yet ready to ascend to heaven and lead them captive. First Peter 3:18–19 says,

> "For Christ also hath once suffered for sins, the just for the unjust, that he might bring us to God, being put to death in the flesh, but quickened by the Spirit: By which also he went and preached unto the spirits in prison."

Next, Jesus was raised from the dead, walked out of the tomb, and was shortly met by Mary Magdalene who came early in the morning to put sweet spices on the body of Jesus. She discovered the empty tomb and two angels there telling her that He had risen. Turning around, she was met by Jesus, but she did not recognize Him and thought He was the gardener. She asked where He placed the body of Jesus. When Jesus spoke, she immediately knew it was Jesus and fell down before Him and started to grab Him around His feet. Jesus told her not to touch Him because He had not yet ascended to His Father in heaven. John 20:17 states,

> "Jesus saith unto her [Mary], Touch me not; for I am not yet ascended to my Father."

Why did Jesus do this? Because He is the perfect unblemished sacrifice for the sins of all of mankind. He must now make a trip to heaven to offer His blood in the holy of holies in the heavenly tabernacle. When He did this, the Father accepted His sacrifice, and now the blood of Jesus blots out all our sins. Jesus then went back to earth (by translation), walked among the people, and was seen by over five hundred witnesses. He also went to meet the disciples and eat with them. Afterward, He ascended to heaven to take His place on the throne of God beside the Father. This was when He led the captives (the Old Testament saints) from paradise in the lower parts of the earth to paradise in heaven. Today, when a saint passes away, that person goes directly to heaven to be in the presence of Jesus. The old paradise is now empty and not needed. So, you see my fellow worker was wasting his time praying the dead out of paradise because it is empty. We need to pray for the living to give their hearts to Jesus Christ and make Him the Lord of their lives. After a person is dead, it is too late to pray for that person's soul.

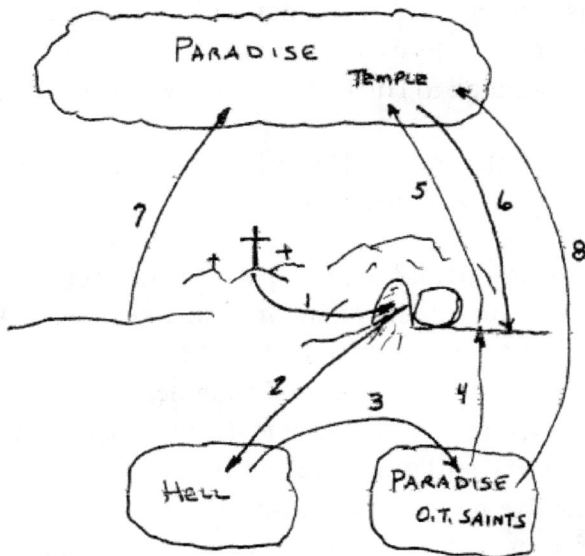

Key for Figure 14 Above:
1. Burial of Jesus in a borrowed tomb (John 19:38)
2. Preached to spirits in Prison (1 Peter 3:19)
3. Preached to Old Testament saints (1 Peter 4:6; Hebrews 10:4; Acts 4:12)
4. Resurrection (Matthew 28:7)
5. Ascended to the temple in heaven (John 20:17)
6. Returned to earth; visited the disciples (John 20:19)
7. Ascension of Jesus to heaven to sit next to the Father (Luke 24:51)
8. Old Testament saints taken to paradise in heaven (Ephesians 4:8–10)

CHAPTER 12

The Rapture

I f the righteous saints are in heaven with Jesus, how does the resurrection mentioned in 1 Thessalonians 4 take place?

> For this we say unto you by the word of the Lord, that we which are alive and remain unto the coming of the Lord shall not prevent them which are asleep. For the Lord Himself shall descend from heaven with a shout, with the voice of the archangel, and with the trump of God: and the dead in Christ shall rise first: Then we which are alive and remain shall be caught up together with them in the clouds, to meet the Lord in the air: and so shall we ever be with the Lord. Wherefore comfort one another with these words. (1 Thessalonians 4:15–18)

Saints who have passed away will have their bodies buried in a grave, but their spirits immediately go to paradise in heaven. When the rapture takes place, their spirits will descend from heaven to reunite with their new resurrected bodies free from all the earthly diseases and afflictions. In fact, they and the saints who are alive will receive a body like Jesus had after His resurrection where He could translate from one place to another in an instant, yet He could partake of food with the disciples. That's how (by translation) Jesus was able to go to heaven to present His blood in the temple there and return to earth the same day. This resurrection is the resurrection of the church, the bride of Christ.

On a side note, people often ask why the United States is not mentioned in prophesies concerning the last days. It would seem that America would be mentioned since we are the greatest world power on the earth at present, but there must be some event that removes America from this exalted position. Your mind might go to a major war where the USA might be defeated and our military reduced to being ineffective, and that is always a possibility, but I think the Bible gives a better answer. I personally believe the rapture of the church and the Christians taken out of the earth in an instant will cause such chaos in every area of our society that the United States will be reduced to a position of a third world country. This then would open the door for the anti-Christ to step out of the shadows and become the world leader. All you have to do is think of all the places Christians serve today, such as doctors, nurses, engineers, the police, firemen and firewomen, politicians, mayors, governors, presidents of large corporations, pilots, ship captains, and many other positions of importance, such as electricians, plumbers, and carpenters; you name it and you will find Christians working in these important jobs. Corporations that produce the military equipment we need, corporations that manage and provide our energy (oil, gas, and electricity). Every facet of our society has Christians in very important positions. One only needs to do the math—the population in America today is around 325 million people, where sixty percent claim to be Christians, that would be 195 million people. Now suppose only one-fourth of them are actually living the true Christian life, not just saying they are Christians—that would be forty-nine million people leaving America instantly. We can't find enough workers for the jobs we have now, so can you imagine all the jobs and services that will be left undone because the Christians are gone? America could be stopped in her tracks as a world leader instantly without a bullet being fired. Also, all the Christians from around the whole earth will be raptured at the same time, causing chaos throughout every country in the world. The world hates the Christians now and persecutes them in many countries, but when we are gone, they sure will see the contribution the Christians have made. The news media no doubt will put a spin on the disappearance of all those people, perhaps saying aliens took them up in a spaceship. No matter what they say, we will be missed. We will be with Jesus in paradise in heaven. Praise the Lord!

THE RAPTURE

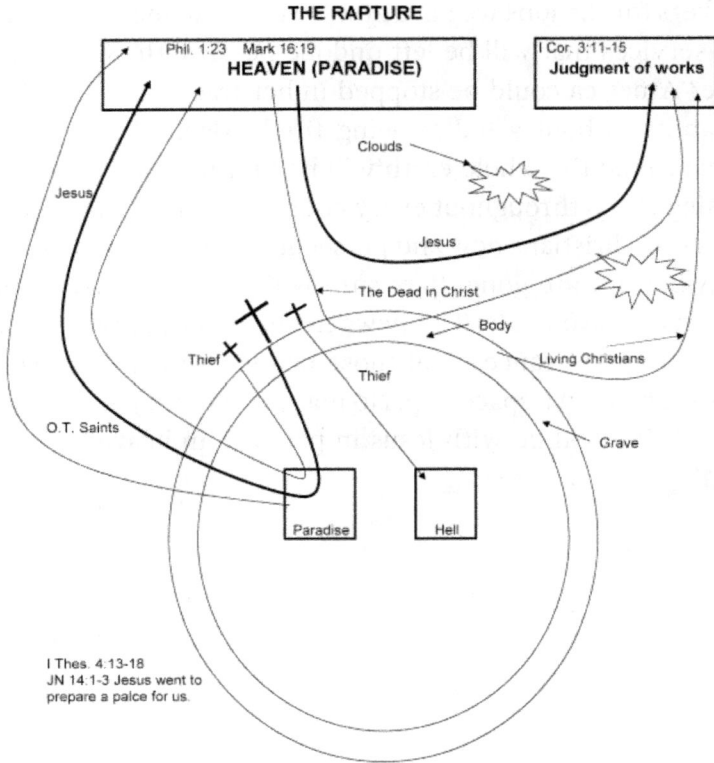

Fig. 15. The rapture of the church.

CHAPTER 13

The Transition

Today, most people who attend Sunday school and church services do not hear a message about the transition. By transition I mean when God reveals something that has never been revealed before (the mystery of the gospel of grace), then the transition from the law to grace. In other words, God has kept the event a mystery for centuries until He deemed it appropriate to reveal it. To understand how these mysteries have been revealed over time, we must start with how God has dealt with mankind over the years of history.

Starting with Adam and Eve, God dealt with the first couple in a personal way, walking in the garden in the cool of the evening and having conversation. From the beginning continuing for 1,946 years, God dealt with mankind as a whole, but mankind was continually disobedient and on a path of degradation. It was at this time in history when Abram was born, plus a few years until God spoke to him calling for him to leave his family and go to a place God would show him. God was about to work with a special people (the Jews). Before the flood of Noah's day, humans did what they desired to do in their own mind. History shows that mankind was on a course of degradation and got to the point where all mans thoughts were evil continually according to Genesis 6:5. God stepped in at that point and decided to destroy all of humankind except for eight souls (Noah's family).

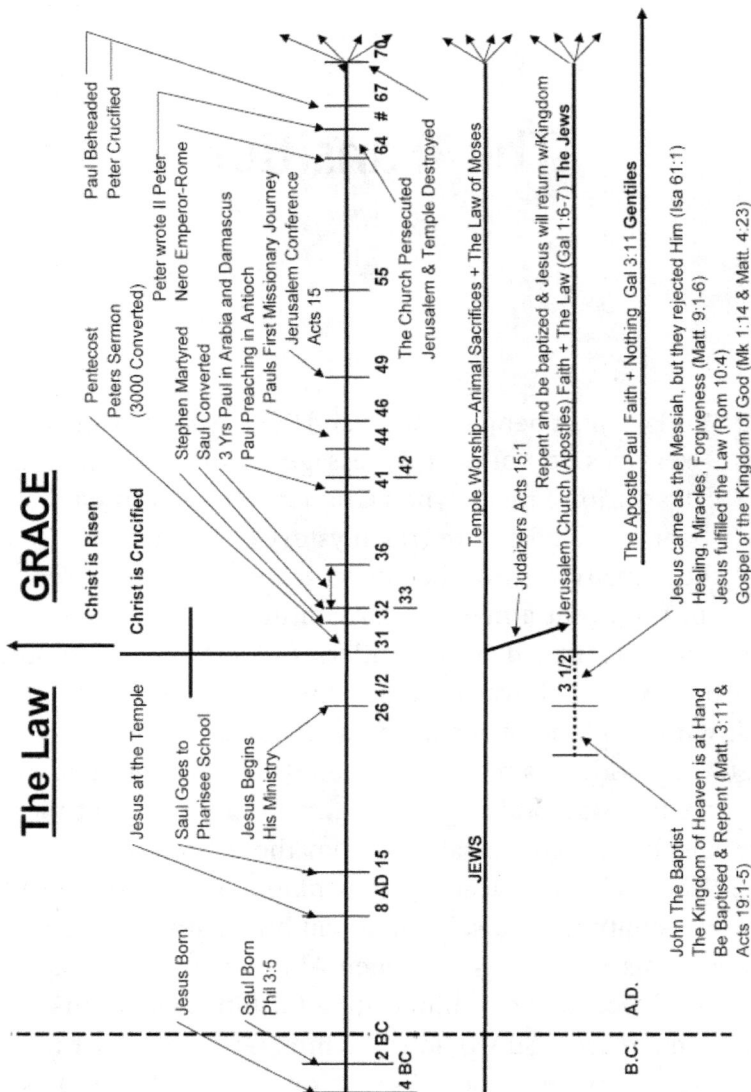

Fig. 16. The transition from the law to grace
(the Church Age begins).

God destroyed the inhabitants of earth, including all living creatures (animals as well) with a great flood that covered the whole surface of the earth. Many today say this was a little regional flood, but you can go up high in the mountains all over the world and find fossils of fish and animals there. The Bible tells us specifically that the waters covered the highest mountain by fifteen cubits or about twenty-two feet, six inches (Genesis 7:20). Noah and his sons (and their wives) began to repopulate the earth, but yet again after about two hundred years, humans fall into idolatry forsaking God. The people build the tower of Babel in rebellion, causing God to confuse their tongues and scatter them throughout the earth. It is interesting to find that all the various civilizations around the world have a history showing there was a great flood. God then decided to work with a select group of people, which He will call His people. They are called the Jews, starting with a man called Abram living in the land of Ur, which was located in the land referred to as Shinar, now modern-day Iraq. Abram was a man of faith, but his family worshipped idols, so God told him to leave Ur and his family and go to a land He would show him. This Abram did by faith and ended up in the land of Canaan. God made a covenant with Abram promising him that He would give the land of Canaan to him and his offspring forever. Later, as a result of a famine in the land, Abraham's grandson Jacob had to move to the land of Egypt where his son Joseph was second in command under the Pharaoh. Joseph was put in charge of managing the food supplies of all the land of Egypt. Jacob and his descendants remained in Egypt for two hundred fifteen years (after Jacob entered Egypt) in slavery until God called a man named Moses to lead them out of captivity, which he did after Egypt suffered ten plagues. The chapter called "The Age of the Earth" explains the years of captivity. God met with Moses on Mount Sinai and gave him the Ten Commandments to help the Israelites worship God and to provide good moral laws to live by. Throughout history, Israel has followed God's laws, then rejected God for idols. They were on and off in their relationship with God. Israel was under the law from Moses until AD 70. Around 4 BC, we know God sent His Son as the Messiah to redeem humankind from their sin nature. The blood Jesus shed by being crucified on the cross at Calvary was and is for the remission of all of mankind's sins, if they would just accept Jesus as their Lord and Savior. After Jesus rose from the grave around AD 31, He, after a time, ascended to heaven where He sits at the right hand of the Father on His throne. The followers of Jesus, the apostles, where charged by Jesus in Matthew 10:5–7 to go only to the lost sheep of the house of Israel (the Jews). Matthew 10:5–7 states,

> "These twelve Jesus sent forth, and commanded them, saying, Go not into the way of the Gentiles, and into any city of the Samaritans enter ye not: But go rather to the lost sheep of the house of Israel. And as ye go, preach, saying, the kingdom of heaven is at hand."

They were not to go to the Gentiles; therefore, they established the Jerusalem church and ministered to only Jews. Israelites converted to accept Jesus as the Messiah took with them parts of the law and began to make circumcision a requirement to be saved. They were called Judaizers. As the number of people accepting Jesus as the Messiah grew, a young man named Saul who was very zealous for God asked permission from the priests at the temple to travel to Damascus (a city in Syria) to arrest the followers of Jesus and bring them before the Sanhedrin for trial. The Sanhedrin was the supreme council of the Jews composed of seventy elders with the high priest as president. On the way to Damascus, Saul was exposed to a bright light from heaven. Jesus spoke directly to Saul, and he fell to the ground under the power and presence of the Lord. Saul immediately knew he was in the presence of God and on holy ground. He cried out, "What would you have me do Lord?" Saul was instantly converted into a believer, and he was blinded. Jesus told him to go to Damascus where He would have a man come and lay hands on him and he would get his sight back, which he did. After this, God the Holy Spirit led Saul into the wilderness in Arabia where God showed him a mystery never before known to mankind, not even the apostles in Jerusalem. Saul remained in the desert for three years under the instruction of the Holy Spirit. Paul stated in Galatians 1:11–24 that he did not receive the gospel he preached from man nor did he consult with the apostles in Jerusalem, but he was taught by God the Holy Spirit. This event marks the beginning of salvation by grace—believing in Jesus's death, burial, and resurrection by faith. No works are required by humans for salvation, just faith. Saul's name was changed by God to Paul (Acts 13:9), and his ministry was to take the gospel of salvation by grace to the Gentiles. When we talk about the transition, it goes like this. The law and temple worship transitioned to the gospel of repentance of John the Baptist, which transitioned to the gospel of the kingdom of heaven under Jesus's ministry and the apostles, and finally to the gospel of grace (Paul's gospel). This transition took place in just around thirty years. In the next chapter, we will look at the mystery revealed to the apostle Paul. Below is a picture of the transition.

THE TRANSITION FROM LAW TO GRACE

	The Law	Gospel of Repentance →	Gospel of the Kingdom →	Gospel of Grace →
Place of Worship	Temple Worship	No Building	Attended the Temple	Established Churches
Leader	The Levi Preisthood	John the Baptist	Jesus & the Apostles	Apostle Paul
Message	Animal Sacrifices & keep the Law	Repent & be Baptised	Receive Jesus as Messiah	Freedom from Law/Saved by Grace
Laws	613 Laws		Kept the Law	Pauls Epistles
Who Message for	Jews Only	Jews Only	Jews Only	Jews and Gentiles

Fig. 17. Transition from law to grace.

CHAPTER 14

The Mystery Revealed

"**M**ystery" means something unknown or not understood, or something hidden. "Mystery" also can mean a secret, which is a mystery because it has not been revealed. In Deuteronomy 29:29 it says,

> "The secret things belong unto the Lord our God: but those things which are revealed belong unto us and to our children forever, that we may do all the words of this law."

God has secrets, and one of the biggest secrets He has kept up until the time of the apostle Paul was the secret that the gospel of grace involved the death, burial, and resurrection of His Son Jesus Christ. It was the beginning of what we refer to as the Church Age. It also was a secret that the gospel would be taken to the Gentile world, that everyone can be saved, Jew and Gentile. It was the end of keeping the law and the sacrificial system. The temple was about to be destroyed by the Roman general Titus in AD 70, and the Jews would be scattered throughout the world. The Jews did not want to hear this new revelation and rejected the gospel by the most part. The Bible says they are blinded, but only for a time. The Jews considered the Gentiles as dogs, and they would have nothing to do with them. Paul was called to take his gospel to the Gentiles, but he always offered it to the Jews first. When we consider what the Old Testament prophets saw, we can see they did not see the church or the Church Age. They also did not see the resurrection of the Messiah. Why didn't the Old Testament prophets see this? Because God kept it from them until the appropriate time for it to be revealed. The Messiah (Jesus) had been crucified, and God's plan to provide the perfect sacrifice had been fulfilled. Now, God was revealing salvation under grace and not by the blood of animals sacrificed, which did not blot out a human's sin, but covered them for a period of one year. The Jews had to go to the temple and offer another sacrifice to stay in right relationship with God. We have been living for about two thousand years in the Church Age under God's grace toward His people and His church.

The Hidden Mystery

In Galatians 1:11, Paul tells us the gospel he preaches was not given to him by man. He did not go down to Jerusalem to be taught by the apostles, but he went into the Arabian desert for three years where God showed him the mystery of the gospel of grace. In Matthew 13:11, it tells us the gospel of the kingdom of heaven was revealed to the apostles but kept from the Pharisees, who were out to get Jesus. There is no mention of the gospel of grace because Jesus had not yet gone to the cross. The gospel of grace is based on the death, burial, and resurrection of Jesus, as the apostle Paul explains in 1 Corinthians 15:1–4. It was revealed to the apostle Paul. Again, in Mark 4:11 and Luke 8:10, Jesus tells the disciples, "And He said," "Unto you, it is given to know the mysteries of the kingdom of God: but to others in parables.' also in Rom 11:25 it states

"For I would not, brethren, that ye should be ignorant of this mystery, lest ye should be wise in your
own conceits; that blindness in part is happened
to Israel, until the fulness of the Gentiles be come
in."

The mystery of the gospel of grace and the Church Age brought
in the Gentiles while the Jews are in blindness to the gospel of
Christ. In Ephesians 3:1–13, it is clear Paul was given the dispensation of the grace of God for the Gentiles. By revelation, Paul
received the mystery (the gospel) of Christ. In the past it has
been hidden, but has been revealed at this time, the time of Paul's
ministry. Ephesians 3:5 reveals that the mystery was not revealed
in other ages; it was hidden. This mystery has now been revealed
to the apostle Paul by the Holy Spirit so that the Gentiles should
be fellow heirs of the same body and partakers of His promise in
Christ through the gospel. In Ephesians 5:32, Paul stated that the
church and Christ are a great mystery. In Ephesians 6:19, Paul
was to boldly proclaim the mystery of the gospel.

Another event hidden from the Old Testament prophets
was the rapture of the church. This is understandable, since the
church and Church Age were hidden from them, the calling out
of the church would also be hidden. In 1 Thessalonians 4:13–18,
a great event for the saints of God is described in detail, the calling out of the church. We refer to it as the rapture of the church.
The word "rapture" is not in the Bible, but a detailed description of the event of calling out the saints (those dead and those
alive) at the time of Christ's return clearly is described, and the
word "rapture" is fitting. In John 5:28–29, Jesus refers to two res-
urrections of the dead. The first resurrection will be the resurrection of the saints. This would be the same mentioned in 1
Thessalonians 4:13–18, which we refer to as the "rapture." Then
in Revelation 20:11–15, there will be a second resurrection after
the thousand-year reign of Christ Jesus where the dead sinners

will be resurrected to stand before God at the white throne judgment. A great multitude of lost souls will be cast into the lake of fire for eternity. Another secret revealed was that the law was fulfilled in Christ Jesus and that His sacrifice on the cross would do away with the need for animal sacrifices. The Jewish world was being turned upside down. Most were unwilling to accept what occurred on Calvary and remained faithful to the law, animal sacrifices, and worship at the temple in Jerusalem. The Jews are still looking for the Messiah to come and are not aware He has come as a lowly servant. When He returns, He will come as a conquering king, for He is the King of kings and Lord of lords. On the road to Damascus some years after the death of Jesus, God saved the most unlikely person to preach the gospel—the apostle Paul. Paul was a Pharisee, and he was very zealous trying to imprison Christians or even have them put to death as in the case of Stephen. Paul was a consenting witness to the stoning of Stephen, holding the coats of those casting the stones. The embryo of the new church under the apostles' leadership was just getting started, and Paul was trying to wipe it out as an instrument of the temple priests. When Paul got saved, he really got saved, and he was just as zealous serving Jesus as he was when he thought Jesus was an imposter. In Ephesians 3:1, we see the change in Paul when he stated,

> "For this reason I, Paul, the prisoner of Christ Jesus for you Gentiles."

Paul referred to himself as a prisoner of Christ. Why? Because his whole life after his conversion was dedicated to Jesus Christ and the spreading of the gospel of grace given to him. When you look at Paul's life after his conversion, you see a man sold out to Jesus. He suffered beatings many times, hunger and thirst, shipwreck, prison, and finally martyrdom in Rome under Nero. In Ephesians 1:2, Paul asked the question,

"If you have heard of the dispensation of grace which was given to me to you."

The dispensation of grace is the description of the Church Age, which has lasted almost two thousand years to date. Paul is at the beginning of a new dispensation called the Church Age. Paul had been assigned by God to take the grace of God to the Gentiles (that's you and me). Paul in Ephesians 3:3 stated,

"How that by revelation he made known to me the mystery."

As I stated before, according to Deuteronomy 29:29, God has secrets. It states,

"The secret things belong to the Lord our God, but those things which are revealed belong to us and to our children forever, that we may do all the words of this law."

So here in Ephesians 3:3, Paul was saying God has revealed to him a secret kept from us until the day it was revealed to him. Now that it has been revealed, it is available for us to live by, and it belongs to us for the purpose of inviting anyone who will to accept Jesus as their Lord and Savior. Jesus will forgive all your sins. Psalm 103:2–4 says,

"Bless the Lord, O my soul, and forget not all His benefits: who forgiveth all thine iniquities; who healeth all thine diseases; who redeemeth thy life from destruction; who crowneth thee with lovingkindness and tender mercies."

Paul said in 1 Corinthians 4:1, "Let a man so consider us, as servants of Christ and stewards of the mysteries of God." Paul was telling us if we will read, we can understand his knowledge in the mystery of Christ. Read what? Read his epistles (his letters to the churches). There were no commentaries in that day, and the New Testament did not exist to learn about this mystery. The Old Testament was available, but it was not revealed there. It was revealed to Paul. We call it revelation knowledge when God opens up the truth of His Word to the individual. Ephesians 1:5 states,

> "[W]hich in other ages was not made known to
> the sons of men, as it has now been revealed by
> the Spirit to His Holy apostles and prophets."

The book of Ephesians was written between 60-64 AD in Rome, which is after the Jerusalem conference held in AD 49, so it is a correct statement to say this mystery has been revealed to the apostles and prophets. In the early days after Paul's conversion and when he was preaching in Antioch, the Jerusalem church was infiltrated with Judaizers (men who were bringing the law into the Jerusalem church operated by the twelve apostles; Judas was not one of them). This came to a crisis when the Judaizers came to Antioch and told the Gentile Christians there, converted by Paul, they could not be saved unless they were circumcised. Acts 15:1 states,

> "And certain men which came down from Judaea
> taught the brethren, and said, except ye be circumcised after the manner of Moses, ye cannot
> be saved."

This greatly upset Paul, and that's when Paul and Barnabas and some others went to Jerusalem to straighten things out. It was a heated conference until Peter stood up an acknowledged how God had led him to Cornelius's house (a Gentile), and he and his family were all saved; therefore, God was doing a new thing by taking the gospel to the Gentiles. Ephesians 3:6 states,

> "[T]hat the Gentiles should be fellow heirs, of the same body, and partakers of His promise in Christ through the gospel."

Do you see how paramount this verse was to the Jews and seemed to go against everything they understood and believed. For a Jew to accept that a Gentile was a coheir of the promise of Christ was huge. Jews thought of Gentiles as dogs. A Jew was not to have anything to do with a Gentile. If a Jew went into a Gentile's house, the Jew would become unclean. Peter did this only because God told him,

> "[W]hat I call clean, don't you call it unclean" (Acts 10:15).

You see, the gospel can bring all nationalities together if they will accept Jesus Christ as their Lord and Savior. All of this is showing us that a great transition was taking place, and God was the one to usher it in at a time of His choosing. God was moving worship of Him from animal sacrifices in the temple, to the apostles ministering to the Jew only, then to Paul's gospel, which is the gospel of grace for all (Jew and Gentile). Paul's gospel is the gospel of believing in the death, burial, and resurrection of Jesus Christ as our Lord and Savior (1 Corinthians 15:1–4). Why did God do away with animal sacrifices at the temple? Animal sacrifices were pointing to a perfect sacrifice that was coming to the earth as promised in Genesis 3:15 where God tells Satan he (Satan) will bruise the heel of Eve's offspring (Jesus). This happened when Jesus was crucified on Calvary. It satisfied the need of removing humanity's sins from their account. Hebrews 10:3–4 states,

"But, in those sacrifices there is a remembrance
again made of sins every year. For it is not possible that the blood of bulls and goats should take
away sins."

This makes it clear that all the animal sacrifices offered at the
temple were only temporary in that the animal's blood only covered a human's sin for one year. Then that person had to repeat
the offering for another year. But when Jesus came, He was the
perfect unblemished sacrifice whose blood does not cover a human's sin but blots out all the sins, never to be brought up again.
Hebrews 9:12:

"Neither by the blood of goats and calves, but by
His own blood he entered in once into the holy
place, having obtained eternal redemption for us."

The holy place here is the holy of holies in the temple located
in heaven. Do you begin to get the picture of how God is intro-
ducing a major change in our worship and salvation? It was all
promised back in Genesis 3:15—the first prophesy of the coming
Messiah to save the world from their sinful nature. The world
today is still having trouble accepting Jesus as Messiah. The
Jewish people do not recognize Jesus as Messiah. They are still
looking for the Messiah. Witnessing to the Jews can be difficult
since they do not believe in the New Testament and do not accept Jesus Christ as Messiah. You can, however, witness to them
from the Old Testament prophesies about Yeshua (Jesus). Isaiah
53 is especially powerful because it is the forbidden chapter for
the Jews. The Jewish rabbis have kept the Jewish population from
reading this chapter because it is a vivid description of our Savior
after He was crucified.

Use the following scriptures to show them Yeshua was prophesied in the Old Testament:

1. Ezekiel 18:4—sin deserves death.
2. Daniel 12:2—sin separates man from God.
3. Isaiah 53—God's provision for humanity's salvation.
4. Daniel 9—the Messiah came before AD 70, before the temple was destroyed.
5. Micah 5—Messiah born in Bethlehem.
6. Isaiah 53—He would die and rise again.
7. Isaiah 49—the Gentiles would come to Him.
8. Ask the Jewish person, "Anyone you know fit these prophesies?" The answer is YES! YESHUA! JESUS!

Just think how much God loves us (His creation). Before the foundation of the world, God knew we would fail Him and would be in need of a Savior. Immediately after man failed, God in Genesis 3:15 stated He would send a Savior to defeat Satan and provide a way for us to get back into fellowship with Him. His love was so great that according to John 3:16,

> "God so loved the world that he sent His only begotten Son, that whoever believes in Him should not perish but have everlasting life."

Yes, God gave His most precious possession in all the universe, His Son, to redeem mankind from the sinful nature inherited from Adam.

CHAPTER 15

Values

According to Funk and Wagnalls dictionary, one meaning of the word "value(s)" is "[s]omething regarded as desirable, worthy, or right, as a belief, standard, or moral precept." I would enhance that by stating Godly values are a moral compass guiding an individual through life on the right track. Where do we find these values? In God's Word, the Bible. When people stray away from those values, usually their life takes a detour down a road of self-inflicted misery.

God in the mainstream of history decided the nation of Israel needed a moral compass to guide them toward righteous living. To that end, God gave Moses the Ten Commandments as listed in Exodus 20:3–17 as follows:

> Thou shalt have no other gods before me. Thou shalt not make unto thee any graven image, or any likeness of anything that is in heaven above, or that is in the earth beneath, or that is in the water under the earth. Thou shalt not bow down thyself to them, nor serve them: for I am the Lord thy God am a jealous God, visiting the iniquity of the fathers upon the children unto the third and fourth generation of them that hate me. . . . Thou

shalt not take the name of the Lord thy God in vain. Remember the sabbath day, to keep it holy. Six days shalt thy labor, and do all thy work; But the seventh day is the sabbath of the Lord thy God: in it thou shalt not do any work, thou, nor thy son, nor thy daughter, thy manservant, nor thy maidservant, nor thy cattle, nor thy stranger that is within thy gates: For in six days the Lord made heaven and earth, the sea, and all that in them is, and rested the seventh day; wherefore the Lord blessed the sabbath day, and hallowed it. . . . Honor thy father and thy mother: that thy days may be long upon the land which the Lord thy God giveth thee. Thou shalt not kill. Thou shalt not commit adultery. Thou shalt not steal. Thou shalt not bear false witness against thy neighbor. Thou shalt not covet thy neighbor's house, thou shalt not covet thy neighbor's wife, nor his manservant, nor his maidservant, nor his ox, nor his ass, nor anything that is thy neighbor's.

Notice the first four commandments require us to honor and worship God and only Jehovah, not other things. The remaining six commandments are moral values we are to exercise in our lives to remain morally pure and righteous before God and honorable before humans. Every one of God's moral values established in the Ten Commandments are just common sense for people to live by and function as a society. They are a moral compass. Would anyone think of taking a journey into a dense forest, on the ocean, or in a desert without a compass? Not if they have any sense. I had a minister once who told me he went hunting in a forest, and eventually he lost his way and could not figure out where he was or how to get out of the forest. This can be very dangerous especially if it is in the wintertime, as you could freeze to death if you had to remain in the forest overnight. The good news is he eventually found his way out to safety. I am afraid there is an increasing number of people who lack a moral compass. Years ago, and even today, there was a movement that espouses "if it feels good, do it." Well, that sounds good, but following that road will lead you into a life of debauchery (gross indulgence of one's sensual appetites), which will end with a ruined life or at least a life not lived to its full potential.

What do people value or esteem highly who follow the "if it feels good, do it" idea? Nothing, because at any moment, they can change what they are willing to do or say without regard of the consequences. They don't care if they say something that hurts or destroys others because what they say is all important to them and their cause of the moment. This can even play out in their actions. They can physically hurt someone without considering the consequences because they don't have a moral compass to guide them to civility in speech or actions. We see this very evident in the congress men and women today where their hate for a president of the opposite party is so great that they are eaten up with hatred. They have lost all civility, and they have destroyed their integrity as leaders of this nation. They go as far as condoning the peaceful protests of American citizens who have been overtaken by rioting thugs. Instead of speaking out against the riots, they continue to call them peaceful protests, which they are not. This is evidence of a nation that has lost its moral compass. Further, if the American people have lost their moral compass, then they will continue to elect these vile representatives, and they will get the government they vote for.

What does all this mean? Friend, if we as a people don't wake up and realize that God is our friend, not our enemy, we are lost as a people and as a nation. Our freedom as a people is at stake. This all boils down to people reestablishing God's value system in government, in our schools, and in our personal lives. I remember an interview one of the national television reporters had with a former president and his wife. In the interview the reporter asked the president, "What are America's values?" The former president was at a loss to give an answer for America's value system. What a sad testament of a national leader who had no value system. Since that time until now, we have seen America slide down the slippery slope of relativism. According to Wikipedia, "Relativism is a family of philosophical views which deny claims to objectivity within a particular domain and assert that facts in that domain are relative to the perspective of an observer or the context in which they are assessed." Relativism means there are no absolute truths as taught in the Bible. Again, this is an attack against the foundational truths of the Bible. In relativism, if you think something is true, then it must be true even if other people state it to be untrue and even if God's Word states it to be untrue.

I believe a good example of this is the theory of evolution as taught in our public schools. The evolutionist and the creationist are looking at the same evidence and coming up with different conclusions. The evolutionist looks at the animals and humans and has concluded that we all have evolved from a single-celled ameba abiding in a pool of goo. After millions and millions of years, the ameba evolved into a fish, then the fish developed legs, walked out of the goo, and became an embryo that eventually became a monkey and millions of millions of years later, started to stand upright, became more and more intelligent, and finally became me and you. The evolutionist believes humans are evolving into better and better people. The humanists believe humans will become so good and so intelligent they will be a god. The evolutionist does not believe in God, nor intelligent design of the universe and humankind; therefore, it is a godless religion. Why do I call it a religion? Because it takes as much faith to believe in the theory of evolution as it does to believe in God as Creator of the heavens and earth and all that is in them, including humans.

The creationist believes what the Bible says about God as the Creator of the heavens and the earth. The creationist believes

God had a design for the universe and for mankind when He created them. We take God at his Word whereas the evolutionist is still looking for proof that their theory is true. The evolutionist will never find it. God's creation is evidence of a Creator of high intelligence and supreme purpose. Romans 1:20 states,

> "For the invisible things of Him from the creation of the world are clearly seen, being understood by the things that are made, even His eternal power and Godhead; so that they are without excuse."

My point is, the evidence God created the universe and all that is in it is obvious, otherwise God would not have said, "[T]hey are without excuse." The evolutionist must discard God altogether with the result of a godless unproven theory. Two groups looking at the same evidence with different conclusions, thus relativism.

By ascribing to relativism, since there are no absolutes, there is the absence of a value system. You see, people can do whatever they feel like doing. If they want to have an affair and go out on their wives, they can. The wives can do the same. If you live close to your neighbor and you want to play loud music offending your neighbor, you can. Your neighbor can do the same and offend you too. Eventually the laws established by the government begin to offend you, and you decide to disobey them as well. When enough people decide to do this, chaos and anarchy break out. Sounds like what is happening today, doesn't it? I hope you see the importance of having good moral values to live by, and God's values are on a high level to guide us in the right direction. I want to close this book with some important truths from God's Word, truths that can change your life if you are away from God or perhaps if you have never had a relationship with Jesus.

Here are some absolute truths from God's Word:

1. All have sinned and come short of the glory of God (Romans 3:23).
2. While we were sinners Christ died for us (Romans 5:8).
3. The wages of sin is death (Romans 6:23).
4. Salvation is for those who believe that Christ Jesus died for your sins on the cross, was buried, and rose again the third day (1 Corinthians 15:4).
5. Salvation is for those who believe (Romans 1:6).
6. God leads us to repentance (Romans 2:4).
7. We must confess Jesus with our mouth (Romans 10:9).
8. Whosoever calls on the name of the Lord shall be saved (Romans 10:13).

If you believe these truths and you want to establish God-given values in your life, pray this prayer asking Jesus into your heart:

Lord Jesus I confess that I am a sinner and have messed up my life. I need for you, through your Word, to guide me on life's path with your values, not the values of the world.

I repent of my sins, and I want you to guide my life from this day forward. Forgive me, Lord Jesus, of all my sins, come into my heart and cleanse me, wash me with your blood, and make me white as snow. I believe you are the Son of God, and right now I accept you as my Lord and Savior, and I accept that according to your Word, I am saved; I am a Christian. I receive your forgiveness. Amen.

If you prayed this prayer with sincerity of heart, I encourage you to find a congregation of believers who are into the Word, and join with them in studying the deeper truths of God's Word. May God bless you and keep you.

About the Author

Don Weidman began his career as a draftsman in the combustible engine industry where he served for approximately nine years. He worked in the automotive lighting industry for thirty eight years serving as an engineer and engineering manager. Don served on several committees with the Society of Automotive Engineers (SAE) from 1990 until his retirement in 2016. Don is now enjoying retirement with woodworking as a hobby and writing this book as a necessity.

Don has been a student of the Word of God for over fifty-nine years and has taught Sunday school classes for over fifty years. During this period of time, he has learned biblical truths he feels strongly about and believes they must be passed on to the next generation of students and to the public who have an interest in learning the deeper truths of the Bible.

The foundational truths of the Word of God are under attack today and must be defended, and that is the reason the author feels this book is necessary.

About the Book

This book was written for the serious student of the Word of God and will take you step-by-step through the six days of creation and the seventh day of rest (the Sabbath) established by God. The acts of creation are presented in a way most theologians have not presented it. It challenges you to think clearly without presupposed ideas. It takes a serious look at the evidence for a young earth and covers a journey from the cross to the tomb, to paradise below, and finally to paradise in heaven. It covers the transition from the law and temple worship to salvation by grace. Finally, it covers the mystery revealed to the apostle Paul.

Preview

This book is meant to educate students everywhere of the foundational truths as they are written in the Bible. We have, since the mid-nineteenth century, been in a battle where so-called scientists, politicians, and schoolteachers, from kindergarten to college professors, have tried to tear down the foundational truths of the Word of God. It appears that academia does not care what God has said. We as Christians have had to deal with the unproven theory of evolution being taught to our children as early as kindergarten when the teacher says, "Today we are going to read about dinosaurs millions and millions of years ago." At that point, the young, impressionable mind has been brainwashed. Mom and Dad and the church must be wrong. The evolutionists have not proven that humans evolved from a one-celled amoeba out of the goo, but it is taught as truth today in public schools. No wonder our nation is turning away from God and becoming a heathen nation.

Then there is the argument used by the evolutionists to justify not having evidence or proof of a species transitioning into another species, saying it is such a slow process that it takes million and millions of years for this to occur. I am interested in what God has to say about this argument. They also say the dinosaurs died out sixty million years ago, which means death had to be present on the earth before Adam was created. The Bible clearly states that death came on the earth as part of the curse when Adam and Eve sinned in the garden. So, the battle lines are drawn. Either the unproven theory of evolution is true or what God has said in His Word is true. This book will cover those subjects in detail as well as other major events such as the transition from law to grace and the mystery revealed. If you as a parent care about what your child is learning in the classroom, then this book is for you.

www.ingramcontent.com/pod-product-compliance
Lightning Source LLC
Chambersburg PA
CBHW060258050426
42448CB00009B/1682